WISDOM

FOR BA (1ST SEMESTER) OF BPSMV

ANJLI SEHRAWAT & ANNU SEHRAWAT

PREAMBLE

WE, THE PEOPLE OF INDIA, having solemnly

resolved to constitute INDIA into a SOVEREIGN

SOCIALIST SECULAR DEMOCRATIC REPUBLIC

and to secure to all its citizens:

JUSTICE , social , economic and political ;

LIBERTY of thoughts , expression , belief faith and worship ;

EQUALITY of status and of opportunity ;

and to promote among them all ;

FRATERNITY assuring the dignity of the individual

and the unity and integrity of the nation ;

WE DO HEREBY GIVE TO OURSELVES THIS CONSTITUTION.

Contents

Foreword

BPS University, KHABPUR has revised the course contents of BA course. This book has been especially written for the new syllabus of paper code : **ENG 101 "Wisdom"**. Some of the distinguishing features of the book are as follows :

- Full coverage of the prescribed syllabus.
- Systematic and sequential arrangement of topics as per the syllabus.
- Lucid and simple language.
- Summery
- Long & Short questions answer
- Grammar

I am sure that this book would be very useful both students and teachers. Suggestions and critical comments for improvement of the book are welcome.

Author

e-mail : annusehrawat8520@gmail.com

9817663033

Preface

I would like to express my special thanks of gratitude to my Teacher **"Monika Mam, Sandeep Sir, Mukesh • Sir, Rashmi Mam, Dr. Prashant Kumar, Mr. Kapil Sir & Dr. Ashok Kumar"** who gave me the golden opportunity to do this wonderful work "write a book" , which also helped me in doing a lot of Research and i came to know about so many new things. I am really thankful to them. Words are short for expressing my gratitude to them.

A special thanks to my friend **Jyoti Dawar** and **Neetu** who always motivate me.

I am also very thankful to all my relatives and friends for their inspiration and encouragement. Words are short for expressing my gratitude to them.

Finally, I am short of words in expressing my gratitude and love to my dear & loving mother ***Mrs. Sushila Sehrawat and father Narender Sehrawat*** who has always inspired and encouraged me in every sphere of my life.

Prologue

SYLLABUS
BPS UNIVERSITY, KHANPUR
BA (1st Semester)
WISDOM
Paper Code : ENG 101
UNIT - 1

1. 'Three questions' by "**Leo Tolstoy**"
2. 'After Twenty years' by "**O Henry**"
3. 'The Refugees' by "**Pearl S. Buck**"
4. 'The Bet' by "**Anton Chekhov**"

UNIT - 2

1. 'The Blind Dog' by "**R.K. Narayan**"
2. 'The Child' by "**Premchand**"
3. 'The Mark of Vishnu' by "**Khushwant Singh**"
4. 'Pigeons at Daybreak' by "**Anita Desai**"

UNIT - 3

1. Sentence and Types of Sentences
2. Part of Speech
3. Adjectives
4. Adverbs

UNIT - 4

1. Paragraph Writing
2. Punctuation Marks

CHAPTER ONE

Three Questions

<u>By Leo Tolstoy</u>

It once occurred to a certain king that if he always knew the right time to begin everything; if he knew who were the right people to listen to, and whom to avoid; and, above all, if he always knew what was the most important thing to do, he would never fail in anything he might undertake.

And this thought having occurred to him, he had it proclaimed throughout his kingdom that he would give a great reward to anyone who would teach him what was the right time for every action, and who were the most necessary people, and how he might know what was the most important thing to do.

And learned men came to the king, but they all answered his questions differently.

In reply to the first question, some said that to know the right time for every action, one must draw up in advance a table of days, months, and years, and must live strictly according to it. Only thus, said they, could everything be done at its proper time. Others declared that it was impossible to decide beforehand the right time for every action, but that, not letting oneself be absorbed in idle pastimes, one should always attend to all that was going on, and then do what was most needful. Others, again, said that however attentive the king might be to what was going on, it was impossible for one man to decide correctly the right time for every action, but that he should have a council of wise men who would help him to fix the proper time for everything.

But then again others said there were some things which could not wait to be laid before a council, but about which one had at once to decide whether to undertake them or not. But in order to decide that, one must know beforehand what was going to happen. It is only magicians who know that; and, therefore, in order to know the right time for every action, one must consult magicians.

Equally various were the answers to the second question. Some said the people the king most needed were his councilors ; others, the priests; others, the doctors; while some said the warriors were the most necessary.

To the third question, as to what was the most important occupation, some replied that the most important thing in the world was science. Others said it was skill in warfare; and others, again, that it was religious worship.

All the answers being different, the king agreed with none of them, and gave the reward to none. But still wishing to find the right answers to his questions, he decided to consult a hermit, widely renowned for his wisdom.

The hermit lived in a wood which he never quitted, and he received none but common folk. So the king put on simple clothes and, before reaching the hermit's cell, dismounted from his horse. Leaving his bodyguard behind, he went on alone.

When the king approached, the hermit was digging the ground in front of his hut. Seeing the king, he greeted him and went on digging. The hermit was frail and weak, and each time he stuck his spade into the ground and turned a little earth, he breathed heavily.

The king went up to him and said: "I have come to you, wise hermit, to ask you to answer three questions: How can I learn to do the right thing at the right time? Who are the people I most need, and to whom should I, therefore, pay more attention than to the rest? And, what affairs are the most important and need my first attention?"

The hermit listened to the king, but answered nothing. He just spat on his hand and recommenced digging.

"You are tired," said the king, "let me take the spade and work awhile for you."

"Thanks!" said the hermit, and, giving the spade to the king, he sat down on the ground.

When he had dug two beds, the king stopped and repeated his questions. The hermit again gave no answer, but rose, stretched out his hand for the spade, and said:

"Now rest awhile – and let me work a bit."

But the king did not give him the spade, and continued to dig. One hour passed, and another. The sun began to sink behind the trees, and the king at last stuck the spade into the ground, and said:

"I came to you, wise man, for an answer to my questions. If you can give me none, tell me so, and I will return home."

"Here comes someone running," said the hermit. "Let us see who it is."

The king turned round and saw a bearded man come running out of the wood. The man held his hands pressed against his stomach, and blood was flowing from under them. When he reached the king, he fell fainting on the ground, moaning feebly. The king and the hermit unfastened the man's clothing. There was a large wound in his stomach. The king washed it as best he could, and bandaged it with his handkerchief and with a towel the hermit had. But the blood would not stop flowing, and the king again and again removed the bandage soaked with warm blood, and washed and re-bandaged the wound. When at last the blood ceased flowing, the man revived and asked for something to drink. The king brought fresh water and gave it to him. Meanwhile the sun had set, and it had become cool. So the king, with the hermit's help, carried the wounded man into the hut and laid him on the bed. Lying on the bed, the man closed his eyes and was quiet; but the king was so tired from his walk and from the work he had done that he crouched down on the threshold, and also fell asleep – so soundly that he slept all through the short summer night.

When he awoke in the morning, it was long before he could remember where he was, or who was the strange bearded man lying on the bed and gazing intently at him with shining eyes.

"Forgive me!" said the bearded man in a weak voice, when he saw that the king was awake and was looking at him.

"I do not know you, and have nothing to forgive you for," said the king.

"You do not know me, but I know you. I am that enemy of yours who swore to revenge himself on you, because you executed his brother and seized his property. I knew you had gone alone to see the hermit, and I resolved to kill you on your way back. But the day passed and you did not return. So I came out from my ambush to find you, and came upon your bodyguard, and they recognized me, and wounded me. I escaped from them, but should have bled to death had you not dressed my wound. I wished to kill you, and you have saved my life. Now, if I live, and if you wish it, I will serve you as your most faithful slave, and will bid my sons do the same. Forgive me!"

The king was very glad to have made peace with his enemy so easily, and to have gained him for a friend, and he not only forgave him, but said he would send his servants and his own physician to attend him, and promised to restore his property.

Having taken leave of the wounded man, the king went out into the porch and looked around for the hermit. Before going away he wished once more to beg an answer to the questions he had put. The hermit was outside, on his knees, sowing seeds in the beds that had been dug the day before.

The king approached him and said, "For the last time, I pray you to answer my questions, wise man."

"You have already been answered!" said the hermit, still crouching on his thin legs, and looking up at the king, who stood before him.

"How answered? What do you mean?" asked the king.

"Do you not see?" replied the hermit. "If you had not pitied my weakness yesterday, and had not dug these beds for me, but had gone your way, that man would have attacked you, and you would have repented of not having stayed with me. So the most important time was when you were digging the beds; and I was the most important man; and to do me good was your most important business. Afterwards, when that man ran to us, the most important time was when you were attending to him, for if you had not bound up his wounds he would have died without having made peace with you. So he was the most important man, and what you did for him was your most important business. Remember then: there is only one time that is important – now! It is the most important time because it is the only time when we have any power. The most necessary person is the one with whom you are, for no man knows whether he will ever have dealings with anyone else: and the most important affair is to do that person good, because for that purpose alone was man sent into this life."

<u>SUMMARY</u>

The three questions were: what was the right time for every action, who were the right people to be with and what was the most important thing to do. He proclaimed that he would give a great reward to the person who can answer his three questions.

A lot of learned men came up with their answers. Unfortunately, their answers did not satisfy the king. So the king decided to consult a wise hermit. He saw the hermit digging the ground and out of compassion, he did it for the hermit. He kept on asking the three questions but the hermit kept silent until hours passed and it was already sunset.

The hermit saw a bearded man running and his hands on his stomach. He was wounded and dying; the hermit told the king about it and they helped the bearded man.

The next day, the king woke up and the bearded man saw him and apologized to him. He admitted that he was an enemy of the king. The bearded man said that he heard about the king going to the hermit so he tried to kill him when he was in his way back home but he failed.

The king asked the hermit once again for his answers to which the hermit said that the most important time is our present because it is the only moment when we have the power to act. The most important person at a moment is we ourselves because the future is unpredictable and the most important business is to be kind and good to others because we have been sent in this world to serve this noble cause.

So this way the hermit tells the king that all the answers are within himself. By helping the wounded man and by spending time with the hermit he gets to know the answer to his questions which he got through self-realization. He learned to do good to others without thinking about ownself.

<u>Reference to Context</u>

Question 1.

In reply to the first question, some said the king must prepare a timetable, and then follow it strictly. Only in this way, they said, could he do everything at its proper time. Others said that it was impossible to decide in advance the right time for doing something. The king should notice all that was going on, avoid foolish pleasures, and always do whatever seemed necessary at that time. Yet others said that the king needed a council of wise men who would help him act at the proper time. This was because one man would find it impossible to decide correctly, without help from others, the right time for every action.

(i) What was the advice of people on making timetable?

(ii) What was the reason of opposing the timetable?

(iii) In their opinion, what the king should do?

(iv) How would the council of wise men be help to the king?

(v) What is a 'council'?

Answer:

(i) They advised him to prepare timetable to complete everything on time.

(ii) A few people opposed it because they felt that it was impossible to decide in advance for doing something;

(iii) The king should avoid pleasure and always be vigilante.

(iv) The council of wise men would give advice to the king to decide correctly for every action.

(v) It is a group of people chosen to give advice.

Question 2.

The hertnit lived in a wood which he never left. He saw no one but simple people, and so the king put on ordinary clothes. Before he reached the hermit's hut the king left his horse with his bodyguard, and went on alone. As the king came near the hermit's hut, he saw the hermit digging the ground in front of his hut. He greeted the king and continued digging. The hermit was old and weak, and as he worked, he breathed heavily.

(i) Where did the hermit live?

(ii) Why did the king choose to wear ordinary clothes?

(iii) What was the hermit doing when the king visit him?

(iv) Why was he breathing heavily?

(v) Convert the adjective for "heavy' into adverb.

Answer:

(i) The hermit lived in a jungle.

(ii) The hermit saw simple people only, so the king put on simple clothes to visit him.

(iii) The hermit was digging the ground in front of his hut when the king visited him.

(iv) He was breathing heavily while digging the grounds, because he was old and weak.

(v) Heavily.

Question 3.

The king turned round and saw a bearded man running towards them. His hands were pressed against his stomach, from which blood was flowing. When he reached the king he fainted and fell to the ground. The king and the hermit removed the man's clothing and found a large wound in his stomach. The king washed and covered it with his handkerchief, but the blood would not stop flowing. The king re-dressed the wound until at last the bleeding stopped.

(i) Whom did the king see when he turned around?

(ii) What happened to the man?

(iii) What did the king do to stop blood flowing?

(iv) Had the efforts of the king to stop blood paid off?

(v) Who is a 'Hermit'?

Answer:

(i) The king saw a bearded man running toward him.

(ii) The man was injured and when he reached the king, he fainted.

(iii) The king washed the wound and covered it with his handkerchief.

(iv) Yes, the efforts of the king had paid off. The king dressed his wound until the bleeding stopped.

(v) Hermit is a person who lives in solitude.

Question 4.

"You do not know me, but I know you. I am that enemy of yours who swore revenge on you, because you put my brother to death and seized my property. I knew you had gone alone to see that hermit, and I made up my mind to kill you on your way home. But the day passed and you did not return. So I left my hiding-place, and I came upon your bodyguard, who recognised me and wounded me. I escaped from him but I should have died if you had not dressed my wounds. I wished to kill you, and you have saved my life. Now, if I live, I will serve you as your most faithful servant and will order my sons to do the same. Forgive me!"

(i) Why did he call the Jing his 'enemy'?

(ii) Where did he decide to kill the king?

(iii) Why did he come out of his hiding place?

(iv) What did body guards do when they recognized him?

Answer:

(i) Write past participle of 'forgive'.

(ii) The king was his enemy as he killed his brother and seized his property. He decided to kill the king on his way back home.

(iii) He waited for long but the king did not come out of the hermit's hut. So when he in his desperation came out of his hiding place.

(iv) The bodyguards attacked him and wounded him.

(v) Forgiven.

<u>Short Answer Questions</u>

Q. 1. What were the three questions after which the story is named?

Ans:- The three questions after which the story is named are: what was the right time to begin something, who was the right person to listen and what was the most important thing to do.

Q. 2. What suggestions were made in answer to the third question?

Ans:- In answer to the third question, some said science will be most important while others suggested warfare and religious worship.

Q. 3. Why did the king go to the wise hermit?

Ans:- The king went to the hermit as he was renowned for his wisdom and the king was unable to get satisfying answers from the others.

Q. 4. How did the king and the hermit help the wounded man?

Ans:- The king washed the wound and covered it with his handkerchief and kept on dressing it until the bleeding stopped completely. The king also offered him water to drink and with the

the help of the hermit brought him inside the hit and allowed him to spend his night there.

Q. 5. What were the hermit's answers to the three questions?

Ans:- The hermit said that the most important time is our present because it is the only moment when we have the power to act. The most important person at a moment is we ourselves because the future is unpredictable and the most important business is to be kind and good to others because we have been sent in this world to serve this noble cause.

Q. 6. Why did the king want to know answers to three questions?

Ans: He wanted to know answers to three questions because of the thought came to his mind that he would never fail if he knew answers to the three questions i.e. what was the right time for every action, who were the most important people and what the most important thing to do was.

Q. 7. Why was the king advised to go to magicians?

Ans: The king was advised to go to magicians to get the answer for his first question. In answer to the first question, i.e. to decide the right time for doing something urgent one must have to look into the future. Since the only magician could do that, the king was advised to go to magicians.

Q. 8. What suggestions were made in answer to the third question?

Ans: There were many suggestions for the third question. In answer to the third question, i.e what is the most important thing to do, some said science will be most important. Others suggested fighting, and some said religious worship.

Q. 9. Did the wise men win the reward? If not, why not?

Ans: No, the wise men did not win the reward. The king got different answers for all the three questions he had asked. He was not satisfied with any of them.

LONG ANSWER TYPE QUESTIONS

Q. 1. What were the hermit's answers to the three questions? Write each answer separately. Which answer do you like most, and why?

Ans: In answer to the king's first question, the hermit said that there is only one important time 'Now' i.e. present. It is the only time when you have the power to act.

In answer to the king's second question, the hermit said that the most important person is the one with who we are at the present.

In response to the king's third question, the hermit answered that the most important thing to do is to do that person good.

I like the answer of the first question the most because time has the supreme power. It can take you to height if you do something good and can also make you fall on the ground if you won't act in presence. One should live and act according to the present.

Q. 2. (i) Who was the bearded man?

(ii) Why did he ask for the king's forgiveness?

Ans: (i) Bearded man was the enemy of the king who swore to revenge him for seizing of his property and putting his brother to death.

(ii) He asked for the king's forgiveness as the king had saved his life. He came there for taking revenge from the king but instead, the king helped him to get better.

Q. 3. How did the king and the hermit help the wounded man?

Ans: The king and the hermit helped the wounded man by providing him the shelter and protected from the army. The king washed and covered the wound of the man with his handkerchief, but the blood would not stop flowing. The king re-dressed the wound until it stopped bleeding. They took him to hut for taking rest and king also gave him fresh water after being relaxed.

Q. 4. How was the wounded man revived and nursed? Why did he ask forgiveness of the Tsar? What did the Tsar do when he had gained the man for a friend?

Ans. A bearded man came running out of the wood and fainted before the Tsar and the hermit. He had a large wound in his stomach and blood was flowing profusely. They unfastened his clothes. The Tsar washed and bandaged the wound again and again until the blood ceased flowing. In this way, the wounded man was nursed and finally revived.

The bodyguard of the Tsar recognized the man as the Tsar's enemy and wounded him severely. It was the Tsar who took utmost care of him to revive his life. He realized that he would have died if he was not looked after by the Tsar. This act of kindness changed the heart of the bearded man. He repented on his act and asked forgiveness.

The Tsar was very pleased to gain the man as a friend. He offered to send his servants and his own physician to attend to him. He also promised to give back his seized property.

Q. 5.How did the Tsar nurse the wounded man?

Ans. A wounded man came running out of the wood and fainted before the Tsar. When the Tsar unfastened the man's clothing with the help of the hermit, he noticed a large wound in his stomach. Blood was flowing abundantly. He washed and bandaged the wound with his handkerchief and with the hermit's towel. Whenever the bandage was soaked with warm blood, he was removing it. Finally, the blood ceased flowing and the man revived. When the man asked for something to drink, he brought fresh water and drank him. The Tsar with the help of the hermit carried him into the hut and lay on the bed. In this way, the Tsar nursed the wounded man.

Q. 6.Why did the bearded man become an enemy of the Tsar? What did the man swear and resolve to do? Why did he ask forgiveness of the Tsar and what did he promise him?

Ans. The bearded man became an enemy of the Tsar because the Tsar executed his brother and seized his property.

The man swore to take revenge on the Tsar for his brother's execution and seizing his property. He also resolved to kill the Tsar on his return from the hermit.

When the man was severely wounded by the bodyguard, it was the Tsar who nursed him carefully and revived his life. He realized that he would have died if he was not looked after by the Tsar. This act of the Tsar changed the wounded man's mind and he asked forgiveness.

The man promised to serve the Tsar as the most faithful slave and he would also employ his sons to do the same.

CHAPTER TWO

After Twenty Years

<u>By O Henry</u>

The policeman on the beat moved up the avenue impressively. The impressiveness was habitual and not for show, for spectators were few. The time was barely 10 o'clock at night, but chilly gusts of wind with a taste of rain in them had well nigh depeopled the streets.

Trying doors as he went, twirling his club with many intricate and artful movements, turning now and then to cast his watchful eye adown the pacific thoroughfare, the officer, with his stalwart form and slight swagger, made a fine picture of a guardian of the peace. The vicinity was one that kept early hours. Now and then you might see the lights of a cigar store or of an all-night lunch counter; but the majority of the doors belonged to business places that had long since been closed.

When about midway of a certain block the policeman suddenly slowed his walk. In the doorway of a darkened hardware store a man leaned, with an unlighted cigar in his mouth. As the policeman walked up to him the man spoke up quickly.

"It's all right, officer," he said, reassuringly. "I'm just waiting for a friend. It's an appointment made twenty years ago. Sounds a little funny to you, doesn't it? Well, I'll explain if you'd like to make certain it's all straight. About that long ago there used to be a restaurant where this store stands-- 'Big Joe' Brady's restaurant."

"Until five years ago," said the policeman. "It was torn down then."

The man in the doorway struck a match and lit his cigar. The light showed a pale, square-jawed face with keen eyes, and a little white scar near his right eyebrow. His scarfpin was a large diamond, oddly set.

"Twenty years ago to-night," said the man, "I dined here at 'Big Joe' Brady's with Jimmy Wells, my best chum, and the finest chap in the world. He and I were raised here in New York, just like two brothers, together. I was eighteen and Jimmy was twenty. The next morning I was to start for the West to make my fortune. You couldn't have dragged Jimmy out of New York; he thought it was the only place on earth. Well, we agreed that night that we would meet here again exactly twenty years from that date and time, no matter what our conditions might be or from what distance we might have to come. We figured that in twenty years each of us ought to have our destiny worked out and our fortunes made, whatever they were going to be."

"It sounds pretty interesting," said the policeman. "Rather a long time between meets, though, it seems to me. Haven't you heard from your friend since you left?"

"Well, yes, for a time we corresponded," said the other. "But after a year or two we lost track of each other. You see, the West is a pretty big proposition, and I kept hustling around over it pretty lively. But I know Jimmy will meet me here if he's alive, for he always was the truest, stanchest old chap in the world. He'll never forget. I came a thousand miles to stand in this door to-night, and it's worth it if my old partner turns up."

The waiting man pulled out a handsome watch, the lids of it set with small diamonds.

"Three minutes to ten," he announced. "It was exactly ten o'clock when we parted here at the restaurant door."

"Did pretty well out West, didn't you?" asked the policeman.

"You bet! I hope Jimmy has done half as well. He was a kind of plodder, though, good fellow as he was. I've had to compete with some of the sharpest wits going to get my pile. A man gets in a groove in New York. It takes the West to put a razor-edge on him."

The policeman twirled his club and took a step or two.

"I'll be on my way. Hope your friend comes around all right. Going to call time on him sharp?"

"I should say not!" said the other. "I'll give him half an hour at least. If Jimmy is alive on earth he'll be here by that time. So long, officer."

"Good-night, sir," said the policeman, passing on along his beat, trying doors as he went.

There was now a fine, cold drizzle falling, and the wind had risen from its uncertain puffs into a steady blow. The few foot passengers astir in that quarter hurried dismally and silently along with coat collars turned high and pocketed hands. And in the door of the hardware store the man who had come a thousand miles to fill an appointment, uncertain almost to absurdity, with the friend of his youth, smoked his cigar and waited.

About twenty minutes he waited, and then a tall man in a long overcoat, with collar turned up to his ears, hurried across from the opposite side of the street. He went directly to the waiting man.

"Is that you, Bob?" he asked, doubtfully.

"Is that you, Jimmy Wells?" cried the man in the door.

"Bless my heart!" exclaimed the new arrival, grasping both the other's hands with his own. "It's Bob, sure as fate. I was certain I'd find you here if you were still in existence. Well, well, well! --twenty years is a long time. The old gone, Bob; I wish it had lasted, so we could have had another dinner there. How has the West treated you, old man?"

"Bully; it has given me everything I asked it for. You've changed lots, Jimmy. I never thought you were so tall by two or three inches."

"Oh, I grew a bit after I was twenty."

"Doing well in New York, Jimmy?"

"Moderately. I have a position in one of the city departments. Come on, Bob; we'll go around to a place I know of, and have a good long talk about old times."

The two men started up the street, arm in arm. The man from the West, his egotism enlarged by success, was beginning to outline the history of his career. The other, submerged in his overcoat, listened with interest.

At the corner stood a drug store, brilliant with electric lights. When they came into this glare each of them turned simultaneously to gaze upon the other's face.

The man from the West stopped suddenly and released his arm.

"You're not Jimmy Wells," he snapped. "Twenty years is a long time, but not long enough to change a man's nose from a Roman to a pug."

"It sometimes changes a good man into a bad one, said the tall man. "You've been under arrest for ten minutes, 'Silky' Bob. Chicago thinks you may have dropped over our way and wires us she wants to have a chat with you. Going quietly, are you? That's sensible. Now, before we go on to the station here's a note I was asked to hand you. You may read it here at the window. It's from Patrolman Wells."

The man from the West unfolded the little piece of paper handed him. His hand was steady when he began to read, but it trembled a little by the time he had finished. The note was rather short.

"Bob: I was at the appointed place on time. When you struck the match to light your cigar I saw it was the face of the man wanted in Chicago. Somehow I couldn't do it myself, so I went around and got a plain clothes

man to do the job.
    JIMMY."

<u>SUMMARY</u>

'After Twenty Years' is a short story by O.Henry about two best friends, Jimmy Wells and Bob, who decide to go down different paths and make a pact to meet at the same place after twenty years.

Bob leaves New York to go try his luck in the West and Jimmy decides to stay and becomes a cop.

The story opens with a cop walking around the deserted streets of New York in the evening, doing his duty, and checking the locks of every establishment and business that he passes by.

He finds a man standing in the doorway of a hardware store. The man has an unlit cigar in his hand. On enquiring, he tells the cop that he is waiting for an old friend who he had promised to meet at the very place 20 years ago before going West.

He tells the cop that he is waiting for Jimmy Wells, his old friend, almost like a brother, with whom he had spent the golden years of his childhood.

While talking to the cop, the man lights his cigar and in that brief illumination, the cop notices that the man has a pale face, a scar near his right eyebrow, and sharp eyes. The glint of a diamond on the man's scarf tells a lot about his riches, and when he pulls out his diamond-studded watch to check the time, the cop comments that he must have done really well in the West.

The man boasts that he has and wishes that his plodder friend has done at least half of what he has achieved. He is sure that his friend - if he is alive, will definitely meet him as promised, no matter what, for his friend is "the truest, stanchest old chap in the world."

The cop goes on his way, the rain starts to fall and the man keeps waiting.

After a few minutes, a man arrives and introduces himself as Jimmy. Bob is happy to find his friend and both men share pleasantries.

Bob notices that Jimmy has changed, in fact, was taller than he remembered. Jimmy says that he grew a bit after 20.

Jimmy insists that since the old restaurant (where they had had their last meal together 20 years ago) is not there anymore, they should go to some other place.

As they pass the street light, Bob looks at his friend's face and says that though 20 years can change a man in many ways, it rarely changes the shape of a man's nose.

He asks if he is Jimmy.

The other man says that he is not and that Bob has been under arrest for the past 10 minutes. He tells him to come with him quietly and hands him a letter, which says:

"Bob: I was at the place on time. I saw the face of the man wanted by Chicago cops. I didn't want to arrest you myself. So I went and got another cop and sent him to do the job. JIMMY."

<u>Short Question Answer</u>

Q.A. Describe the scene in the beginning of the story.

Ans. A policeman can be seen on duty in an area. He is on foot patrol. It is 10 p.m. The cold wind is blowing. The area seems deserted.

Q.B. Was the place a business centre only?

Ans. Yes, the place was a business centre. The author has mentioned a cigar store and an all-night lunch counter.

Q. C. What kind of characters does the story "After Twenty Years" have?

Ans. There are three characters in the story "After Twenty Years".

· One is Bob who is a true and sincere friend. He want to full fill his promise at any cost.

· His friend Jimmy is dutiful and honest person. He gives preference to duty over friendship.

· The third character who comes to arrest Bob is also a police officer.

Q. D. What is the most significant happening in the story to be analyzed?

Ans. The most significant happening in the story is when Jimmy Wells sends a police officer in plain clothes to arrest Bob.

Q. E. What is the climax of the story "After Twenty Years"?

Ans. Bob identifies that the man he is talking to is not his friend. Actually, the man is a police officer in plain clothes. He gives Bob a letter from Jimmy. Bob learns from the letter that the police officer whom he met earlier was Jimmy, his old friend.

Q. F. How would you describe Jimmy and Bob's personalities in the story?

Ans. Jimmy and Bob are close friends. Jimmy is an honest police officer. When he comes to know that his friend is a criminal, he does not have the courage to arrest him himself. He sends another policeman to arrest Bob. For him duty is more important than friendship. As far as Bob is concerned, he is a true friend. He want to fulfill his promise at any cost.

Q. G. The ending of "After Twenty Years" fill the reader with poignancy, (Strong effect of feeling -sad) making the story effective. Discuss?

Ans. The reader expects that Bob and Jimmy Wells, the two close friends, would meet each other after long separation. They would share their experiences of the past twenty years. But instead, the ending of the story fills the reader with poignancy when one of the friends is arrested by police. In spite of the tragic end, the author makes the story very effective. Bob is not arrested by Jimmy Wells directly. Jimmy sends another police officer to arrest Bob.

Q. H. How does the writer prepare for the end of the story?

Ans. The writer prepares for the end of the story contrary to the expectations of the readers. The story begins very interestingly. Two close friends Bob and Jimmy meet each other after twenty years. Bob does not recognize Jimmy in the police uniform. After Jimmy's departure, another police officer in plain clothes comes whom Bob considers to be his Jimmy. The police officer arrests Bob because he is wanted in Chicago.

Q. I. What did Bob share with the cop about their friendship?

Ans. Bob shared with the policeman his strange appointment made twenty years ago. He also shared the details of their childhood days and how they were raised in New York.

Q. J. What are the strengths and weaknesses of Jimmy Wells from Bob's point of view?

Ans. Strengths: Jimmy Wells is very shrewd. He has sharp memory. He can recognize his friend as soon as he sees his face in the cigar light. He is duty bound.

Weakness: He is very cordial and soft natured person. Though his friend is a criminal wanted in Chicago, he could not arrest him. Hence he sent another cop to do the duty.

Q. K. Was Bob hopeful of his friend's arrival? How do you know?

Ans. Yes, Bob was hopeful of his friend's arrival. The lines "I'll give him half an hour at least. If Jimmy is alive on earth he'll be here by that time" reveal his hopefulness of his friend's arrival.

Q. L. How did the cop come to understand that Bob had been successful in the West?

Ans. Bob pulled out a handsome watch having the lid set with small diamonds. Then the patrolman came to know that Bob had been doing well.

Q. M. Bob's life in the West was not a bed of roses. Give reasons.

Ans. Bob had to compete with some of the intelligent people going to get his pile. He has to manage with the police for the crimes he had committed. He lived with stress and fear that he might be arrested at anytime by the police of West.

Q. N. Why didn't Jimmy Wells, being a cop himself, arrest Bob?

Ans. Jimmy Wells is very cordial with everyone, especially with Bob. He has no willingness and guts to arrest his most intimate friend. Hence he could not arrest Bob.

Q. O. Who do you think has been more successful between the two? Give reasons.

Ans. I think Patrolman Wells has been successful between the two. He has done his duty. He knows his responsibilities. Being a sincere friend he is not able to arrest his most intimate friend. He sent another cop in plain clothes to do the work.

<u>Long Questions Answer</u>

Q. A. Compare and contrast the character of Jimmy Wells and Bob with suitable references from the story to support your view.

Ans. "After Twenty years" by O. Henry is an interesting story with a twist at the end. A 38-year old Bob is waiting at the door of a hardware store in New York to meet his friend Jimmy wells. A policeman is on patrol duty. He asks Bob why he is standing there. Bob tells the cop that he (Bob) is waiting to meet his friend Jimmy Wells. He says that they make a promise to meet at the same place at the same time on the same date after twenty years, before parting. Bob tells the policeman that he (Bob) has kept his promise. Bob is sure that Jimmy Wells will surely come and meet him. After listening to the story, the cop walks away. Twenty minutes later, a tall man in plain clothes comes to meet Bob. Bob thinks him Jimmy Wells. Later Bob identifies that the man he is talking to is not his friend. Actually, the man is a police officer in plain clothes. He gives Bob a letter from Jimmy. Bob learns from the letter that the police officer whom he met earlier was Jimmy, his old friend. Since Bob is a criminal wanted by the Police, Jimmy Wells does not want to arrest his intimate friend. So he has sent another police officer to do the work.

Here Bob is a criminal. But he is a true friend. He wants to fulfill his promise at any cost. On the other hand, his friend Jimmy Wells is an honest police officer. When he comes to know that his friend is a criminal, he does not want to arrest him himself. He has sent another policeman to arrest Bob. For him duty is more important than friendship.

Q. B. 'Means should justify the end.' Explain this adage with reference to O. Henry's story.

Ans. "Means should justify the end" is a well-known proverb. means = method, end=aim. Your aim should be noble, and at the same time the method should also be honest. The aim of a short story is to give aesthetic pleasure to the readers. There should be just two or three characters and the narrative should be brief. Now in the short story "After Twenty years" O. Henry employs only three characters. Two friends agree to meet after 20 years. When they meet one of them is a criminal and the other is a police officer. The police officer is duty-conscious and sends another police officer to arrest his friend. Thus the story has a surprise ending; it gives pleasure to the reader. So the shore story justifies the statement.

"Means should justify the end.

Q. C. 'Tell me who your friends are and I shall tell you who you are'. How will you explain this statement in the light of Jimmy's and Bob's friendship?

Ans. "Tell me who your friends are, and I shall you who you are"--- is common statement. If somebody has bad friends then he (she) is a bad person. If somebody has good friends, he is a good person. But this statement and may twisted. sometimes

A non-vegetarian and a vegetarian may be good friends!!

The short story "After Twenty Years" disproves the proverbial statement of the friends, one is a criminal and the other is a police officer. But the title is meaningful ----"After Twenty Years" They were good friends twenty years ago. But time has changed their characters.

Q. D. To your shock, you find out that your close friend is indulging in some wrong activity. Will you avoid him/her or try to correct him/her? Give reasons for your answer.

Ans. If I find my close friend indulges in some wrong activity, I shall definitely correct him. It is my moral duty. I am bound to do. If any harm is done we should not ignore it. When my close friend does any wrong activity

I can't bear it. For instance let us take my friend smokes and consumes liquor. First of all I don't advise him. For advise is a hatred form to any one, I shall give him live examples from the people who are affected worst. I should make him understand that other people are also affected by his act. It is my duty. Thus I will try to wear him of the bad habit.

Q. E. What would you do in this situation, if you were Jimmy Wells? Substantiate your reason.

Ans. If I were Jimmy Wells I would not send plain clothes cop to arrest Bob. Instead I would arrest him on the spot as soon as I knew that he was the criminal wanted in Chicago. My policy is duty first and friendship next. I stick to my principle even if I face any hurdles. I shall try to be sincere till the dooms day. For, while I go away and try to find another police officer, Bob may become tired of waiting and he may go away. Therefore as soon as Bob lights up his cigar and I identify him as a notorious criminal in New York. I would arrest him before he could have any chance of escaping.

Q. F. What is the moral of the story?

Ans. The short story "After Twenty years" portrays two different characters. Bob is a criminal; he has earned a lot of money. But he has no home, no peace of mind. He is always by the fear that he may be arrested by the police any time. On the other hand, his friend Jimmy Wells is a police officer. He is honest, simple and duty-conscious. Though the two men were friends in their boyhood, now Jimmy Wells sends another police officer and gets Bob arrested.

The moral of the story: Duty is more important than friendship.

Q. G. Who is Jimmy Wells? (OR) Sketch the character of Jimmy Wells.

Ans. Jimmy wells is a police officer in New York. On a dull cold evening he is doing his duty. He walks with a straight looking face and steady steps. As he nears the door of a hardware store, he meets a man. That man is Bob who tells Jimmy Wells about the promise of meeting here made between himself and his friend twenty years ago. Now Jimmy Wells is the friend. When Bob lights up his cigar, Jimmy realizes that Bob is notorious criminal and he is wanted by the police. Jimmy could have arrested Bob on the spot. But Jimmy recalls their early friendship and therefore sends another police officer to arrest Bob.

Thus Jimmy Wells is duty-conscious. He places duty above friendship.

CHAPTER THREE

The Refugees

By Pearl S. Buck

The refugees were walking in a city where they were looked upon as an unwelcome crowd who would create many problems for the original residents. This city which was the capital of their country, was just a few hundred miles away from their own lands, but they felt like outsiders here. They had to leave their lands because of sudden and unexpected floods caused by a big breach in the dikes. While walking on the concrete roads these refugees did not look at anything although many things were quite new to them. They were too hungry and weak to take any active interest in new sights and sounds. They were provided shelter in large camps outside the new capital's city wall.

The refugees would pour in large numbers and usually produced bitterness in city dwellers who would feel disgusted at their sight. Their bitterness was caused by their fear that the presence of these hungry crowds will create many problems for them. This made them hostile and they would often shout rudely at many of the beggars. It also made people merciless in paying smalls fares to rickshaw-pullers. Some of the refugees would pull rickshaw at a much cheaper price and caused competition; some would try their luck in every possible unskilled profession, while others would bend to begging. All this made the city dwellers look upon them as a big nuisance and tended to close their hearts to their suffering.

These refugees had to face penury because of a natural calamity. They were otherwise very proud and self-respecting people and felt ashamed of themselves when they were forced by their helpless condition to take resort to begging. They were tall and strong, wearing clothes made up of dark blue cotton stuff. Their clothes were cut in an old-fashioned way and had long sleeves. Their coats were also long and full. The smocked apron of men had strange, complicated and yet beautiful designs while women had bands on their heads wrapped like kerchief. Every man carried clean and well made clothes and some bedding in two baskets which hung from a pole across his shoulders. There were cooking utensils on each basket but there was no sign of food being cooked in them. A close look at their faces showed that they were homeless, sad and had lost hope of surviving for long, but they bore their difficult situation with patience and courage.

One of the refugees, the last one in the long procession, was an old man who had a wrinkled face and a weak body. Like other refugees, he also carried a load of two baskets – one had a quilt with a cauldron on it while the other had another quilt but no cooking utensil placed on it. He was tired and breathing heavily because the load was quite heavy for the old man. He stopped and after putting his load down, sat down to restore his strength. A passer-by stopped by, felt pity and offered him a bit of money so that the old man could eat noodles and save himself from being starved. But the old man had his dignity and self-respect and did not put his hand out to receive the alms. He told the passer-by that he was not a beggar and had fertile land at home. The passer-by, without paying much attention, dropped the money into the old man's smocked apron and went away after making a sympathetic comment which also carried a tinge of dry humour.

A vendor was selling noodles close-by. He asked the old man whether he would like to buy a big or small bowl of noodles. The old man saw the two coins and said that one small bowl would be sufficient for him. The vendor felt surprised at this preference for a small bowl even when the old man was very hungry. The vendor prepared a small bowl and after handing it over to the old man waited to see who would eat it.

The old man rose with an effort and with the bowl went to the other basket. The vendor watched the old man pulling the quilt away and noticed a little boy with a sunken face. The old man, with great love and care, lifted up the little child's head and made him swallow the food. It was his grandson. After covering the little soul affectionately, the old man licked the little bowl and finished even the last trace of food on it. This was his only meal. When the old man returned the bowl to the vendor and ordered nothing more, he reminded the old man that he still had money to buy another bowl to save himself from hunger. The old man, however, declined to buy any more because he wanted to keep the rest of the seed purchase money. He decided to return to his native land, sow seeds and grow crops. He gave more priority to his obligation to grow new crops on his land than to remove his hunger by buying a bowl of noodles for himself with the silver coin he had with him. He added that he would not take care of his own life in an effort to make his grandson's life easier and healthier. He picked up his load again and began to walk on his old, shaky legs again. The attitude of the old man reveals the integrity and optimism that can keep the peasantry moving even in the most difficult and insufferably painful situation.

<u>The character sketch of The old man in The Refugees</u>

The old was very weak such that his steps were infirm. But he was also hard working and self-respecting person. He had his dignity and never sought help from others. He did neither beg nor extend his hand to receive alms offered to him by the generous passer-by. Looking at him a passerby took pity on him and offers him one silver coin and a copper penny. But the old man had his dignity and self-respect and did not put his hand out to receive the alms. The old man replied "I did not beg of you, we have good land and we have never been starving like this before". The passer-by, without paying much attention, dropped the money into the old man's smocked apron and went away after making a sympathetic comment which also carried a tinge of dry humour.This incident shows how self-respecting and morally strong the old man really was.

And their life was filled with conflicts because of flood. Even the seeds he saved for planting, people ate because of hunger. The old man said "Sir we have no seed left even, we have eaten our seed. I told them we cannot eat the seed. But they were young and hungry they ate it."

The vendor was selling noodles close-by. He asked the old man if he'd like to buy a big or tiny bowl of noodles. The old man saw the two coins and said that one small bowl would be enough for him. The vendor was shocked by this desire for a small bowl even though the old man was really hungry. The vendor prepared a small bowl and, after handing it over to the old man, waited to see who was going to eat it.

The old man rose with an effort and with the bowl went to the other basket. The vendor watched the old man pulling the quilt away and noticed a little boy with a sunken face. The old man, with great love and care, lifted up the little child's head and made him swallow the food. It was his grandson. After covering the little soul affectionately, the old man licked the little bowl and finished even the last trace of food on it. This was his only meal.

When the old man returned the bowl to the vendor and ordered nothing more, he reminded the old man that he still had money to buy another bowl to save himself from hunger. The old man, however, declined to buy any more because he wanted to keep the rest of the seed purchase money. He decided to return to his native land, sow seeds and grow crops. He gave more priority to his obligation to grow new crops on his land than to remove his hunger by buying a bowl of noodles for himself with the silver coin he had with him. He added that he would not take care of his own life in an effort to make his grandson's life easier and healthier. He picked up his load again and began to walk on his old, shaky legs again. The attitude of the old man reveals the integrity and optimism that can keep the peasantry moving even in the most difficult and insufferably painful situation.

<u>Short-Answer Questions</u>

Question.1. '... suddenly and by some unaccountable force...' What could have forced the refugees to leave their land?

Answer. The refugees were land owning farmers at a place a few hundred miles away from the new capital. They had to leave their land unexpectedly because the river rose and broke its dikes. This resulted in a sudden and unexpected calamity of floods on their lands and they were forced to leave their land at once.

Question 2. Were the refugees really alien to the new capital?

Answer. No, literally they were no foreigners because they were citizens of the country of which the city was the new capital; but as refugees, they were aliens to the new capital. They were being looked down upon and sneered at by the city dwellers. This made them feel as if they were aliens having nothing in common with the city-dwellers. Their desperate condition also made them feel like those who had no interest in the world around them just before their death.

Question 3. Name any two things in the new capital which the refugees had never seen before.

Answer. The refugees were country side people and had never witnessed the new capital. There were numerous things which had they never seen before. They were accustomed only to country roads and fields, but presently they were walking on the concrete sidewalk. Also there were automobiles which they observed for the first time in their lives.

Question 4. Why did the refugees look at nothing and pass as in a dream?

Answer. The refugees belonged to a place which was few hundred miles away from the new capital. They were desperate as they had to abandon their land and homes due to the unexpected floods that ruined them completely. They were strangers and homeless; they were without money and jobs. Their sad and uncertain life made them lost in dreams and hence they paid no heed to anything.

Question 5. 'Neither did any look at them.' Why?

Answer. The refugees came in the form of large crowds in the new capital after leaving their homes. But their coming to the city in such large numbers was not liked by the city-dwellers. They were treated as aliens and looked down upon by most of the on-lookers. The people in the city would sneer at them and see in them a threat to their own comforts and needs. They disliked their presence and this attitude of distrust and dislike made them indifferent to their suffering and even killed their natural curiosity in them. They did not show any interest or fellow-feeling and did not even care to look at them.

Question 6. What was the reaction of city dwellers who noticed the refugees?

Answer. The city dwellers treated these refugees as outsiders and disliked their presence. Some of the refugees turned to begging while others tried to get any kind of unskilled work available in the city to earn enough for bare survival. Most of them started pulling rickshaw. The city dwellers, as a result, thought them to be a threat to their livings and life. They developed an attitude of hostility and contempt because of their fear of the adverse effect on their own lives. The beggars were shouted away and the others distrusted and feared.

Question 7. Why did the regular rickshaw-pullers curse the refugees?

Answer. Some of the refugees started begging while others began doing unskilled jobs. Most of them started pulling rickshaws at lower fares than those prevailing before their arrival. This created a situation of cut-throat competition and the already existing rickshaw-pullers had to lower down their charges even if it failed to provide them enough to make their two ends meet. That is why the regular rickshaw pullers cursed the refugees.

Question 8. What showed that the refugees were all from one region?

Answer. The refugees were wearing the same kind of clothes. Their clothes were made of the same dark blue cotton. Their clothes were also made in the same old fashioned way with their shirts having long sleeves and their coats being long and full. They all wore complex and beautifully designed aprons with the same type of folds and knots. They were tall and strong although the women's feet were bound. They carried two baskets with similar belongings. These were clear indications that they were from the same place.

Question 9. What load did the old man carry in the two baskets on his sling?

Answer. The old man with the wrinkled face carried, like all other refugees, two baskets slung on his shoulders. In one basket there was a quilt with a big cooking utensil placed on it. But unlike most other refugees, the old man had only a quilt in the other basket with no cooking utensil on it. We come to know later on that his little grandson was lying safely in this second basket under the quilt.

Question 10. What money did a man passing by give to the old refugee?

Answer. When the old man sat down to take rest for a while, a kind-hearted man who was passing by stopped by and pitied his hard condition. He offered the tired soul the money he had earned that day. He searched his pocket and brought out a silver coin from there. He hesitated for a while and then added a copper penny to it. He dropped this money in the man's apron since he did not extend his hand to take it from him. The passer-by then moved on.

Question 11. Why did the old man order only one small bowl of noodles?

Answer. The old man was given a silver coin and a copper penny by a kind-hearted passer-by who wanted to see him eat noodles. But he old man ordered one small bowl of noodles only in order to save the rest of the money. He wanted to buy seeds, sow them in his fields and get crops from them when he returned home. He was a man of strong character who wanted to secure some earning for his grandson. Even though he was very hungry, he did not want to spend silver coin on his own food.

Question 12. What was the old man's reply when the vendor reminded him: 'But you have the silver bit'?

Answer. The old man ordered one small bowl of noodles only so that he could save money. When the vendor reminded him that he had a silver coin with which he could order a large bowl of noodles for himself, the old man told him that he would buy seeds with the saved money, sow them in his fields and get crops. The old man wished to regain his earlier prosperous condition in this way.

Question 13. Which line suggests that even the vendor was moved to pity at the sight of the old man?

Answer. The vendor who was selling noodles felt pity and sympathy for the ragged old man who was quite hungry but who even in this desperate condition showed moral courage not to spend the silver coin given to him by a sympathetic passer-by. He was touched by the miserable condition of the old man and said that if he himself was not so poor he would have given a bowl of noodles to him without charging anything for it. He expressed his helplessness and sorrow over the situation by saying that he could not serve noodles to a person who had a silver coin with him.

Question.14 The passer-by's generosity in giving money to the old man has been termed as 'bitter heartiness.' Why?

Answer. Although the passer by was a kind and generous fellow yet there was bitterness in his tone and manner. He, along with other local people, felt a general distrust and fear of the refugees which despite his pity for the old man, he could not fully overcome. Without being asked or begged for he dropped the money into the old man's smocked apron in this mixed state of mind which has been described by the author as 'bitter heartiness' and hurriedly went his way.

Question.15. 'When he saw the silver, he would not put out his hand.' What trait of the old man's personality is reflected by this?

Answer. The old man in "The Refugees" was a self-respecting person. He had his dignity and never sought help from others. He did neither beg nor extend his hand to receive alms offered to him by the generous passer-by. This incident shows how self-respecting and morally strong the old man really was.

Long-Answer Questions

Question.1. Is 'The Refugees' a didactic story? What message does it convey?

Answer. "The Refugees", written by Pearl S. Buck is a didactic story with a clear message attached to it. Through the courage and determination with which most of the refugees conduct themselves even under severely trying conditions, the author stresses the need for protecting our self-respect and dignity at all costs. This is very clearly brought out in the story through the example of the old man who is trying his utmost to save his grandson without compromising his self-respect in any way. This old man refused to bow before the adverse circumstances. He had no food and no money yet he neither begged nor extend his hand to receive money from a passer-by who wanted to give it to him out of pity for him. He decided to save the silver coin placed by the passer-by in his apron in order to buy seeds and grow crops in his fields instead of spending it on a bowl of noodles for himself.

The old man is a symbol of struggling humanity. He faces life's challenges boldly without losing dignity and self-respect. The story underlines the beauty of his determination and optimism which impel him to plan for a better future even when he is placed in a very desperate situation. "The Refugees" teaches us not to give up hope and courageously face adverse circumstances and to look forward to a better future for oneself.

Question.2. Could one call the old refugee man a beggar? Comment.

Answer. No, we cannot call the old man a beggar because he exhibited no signs of a behaviour which would justifiably put him in this category. He was, no doubt, without food and money and had no shelter yet he did not lose his self-respect. He affirmed his dignity by not extending his hand forward for the money offered to him by a passer-by out of a sense of pity for him. He was frail and had to abandon his home and land because of the sudden floods that devastated the village completely. And even in this difficult situation, he showed determination and courage by doing all he could to save his little grandson's life.

In the new capital city where he had reached along with other people of his village, a passer-by took pity on his condition and dropped money in his apron. The old man told him that he was not a beggar. He added that he had good lands but got ruined because of the unexpected floods. He was not led by the force of hunger and desperation to extend his hand for the alms offered to him by the passer-by. These gestures of the old man are ample indications that he was not a beggar but a proud and self-respecting person who tried to preserve his dignity even in very adverse circumstances.

Question.3. 'These were men and women of which any nation might have been proud,' says the narrator about the refugees Why?

Answer. "The Refugees" by Pearl S. Buck is a pathetic tale of those unfortunate people who became victims of a natural calamity of an unexpected flood. They were farmers who had to abandon their village when the river broke its dikes. They tried to stick to their place till the very last moment. They were tall and strong and stayed by their land until starvation forced them to look for their livelihood elsewhere. They were not ordinary people and had never witnessed degrading poverty in their lives. Even in very adverse circumstances they tried to find work for themselves and most of them did not take resort to begging to save themselves from starvation. Any nation could feel proud of citizens who displayed so much of moral stamina and determination. The old man in the story is a symbol of struggling humanity. Although adverse conditions brought these people to penury and compelled them to do humble jobs in order to earn their living, they did not want to be a burden on others. The old man in the story was a dignified person who had a desire to regain his prosperous past. That is why the writer has said that any nation might have been proud of these people.

Question.4. What are the most important concerns of the old starved man and how does he show them in his behaviour?

Answer. The most important concerns of the old wizened man are to keep his dignity, look after his little grandson and to regain the prosperity that he had lost. He was uncertain of his life in the new capital. Being old and tired, he rested for a while to relax and regain his strength. In the mean time a passer-by felt pity on his miserable condition and offered him some money. The old man did not put out his hand to receive the alms to avoid being called a beggar.

He did order one small bowl of noodles to feed his starving grandson who was the only other survivor in his family. The infant was kept warm and safe in the quilt and fed with utmost love and care. He exhibited little concern for his own self and cared more for his grandson and his lands. He decided to keep the rest of the money to buy seeds with which he could grow crops in his field and bring back his lost prosperity. He did not surrender before life's difficulties and decided to face the challenges which came up before him boldly. The old man in "The Refugees" is a person with moral stamina and courage. Any nation will feel proud of having citizens like him.

Question.5. Describe the physical and mental condition of the refugees in the new capital.

Answer. The refugees, who were pouring in hordes in the new capital, were victims of a natural calamity. They had lands and homes, but due to unexpected floods, everything got ruined and they had to leave their native land to become refugees in the capital city where they were distrusted and feared by most people. They were wearing the same type of clothing made up of blue cotton stuff. They wore strange, complicated and beautifully designed aprons. They all were tall and strong although the women's feet were kept bound.

All the refugees were tired and exhausted. The state of prolonged starvation had created a tense situation which prevented them from taking active interest in the new objects they saw in the city. They tried to do diverse jobs to make their two ends meet. Some of them started to beg, some started pulling rickshaw while others tried their hands at any unskilled jobs they could find. They were poor and lived in great camps outside the city wall. They led a miserable life but showed great determination and courage even in these adverse conditions.

CHAPTER FOUR

The Bet

By Anton Chekhov

Anton Chekhov

First published in an 1889 edition of the St. Petersburg-based newspaper Novoye Vremya (Новое время), Anton Chekhov's "The Bet" ("Пари") is a short story about a bet made between a banker and a lawyer. During a dinner party in November 1870, a wealthy banker claims that capital punishment is more humane than life imprisonment. The younger lawyer counters that to live under any circumstance is always better than death. The two debate and make a bet: if the lawyer can live in solitary confinement, the banker will give him two million rubles. The lawyer agrees to stay isolated in a lodge in the banker's garden for fifteen years. Over the course of those fifteen years, the lawyer fervently reads and studies. In the meantime, the banker's wealth begins to dwindle and he must make a rash decision in order to save his money. Characteristic of his stories and plays, Chekhov ends the short story on an ambiguous note as the lawyer emerges from his confinement with a new understanding of the world and a complete rejection of materiality.

The Bet

It was a dark autumn night. The old banker was walking up and down his study and remembering how, fifteen years before, he had given a party one autumn evening. There had been many clever men there, and there had been interesting conversations. Among other things they had talked of capital punishment. The majority of the guests, among whom were many journalists and intellectual men, disapproved of the death penalty. They considered that form of punishment out of date, immoral, and unsuitable for Christian States. In the opinion of some of them the death penalty ought to be replaced everywhere by imprisonment for life. "I don't agree with you," said their host the banker. "I have not tried either the death penalty or imprisonment for life, but if one may judge a priori, the death penalty is more moral and more humane than imprisonment for life. Capital punishment kills a man at once, but lifelong imprisonment kills him slowly. Which executioner is the more humane, he who kills you in a few minutes or he who drags the life out of you in the course of many years?"

"Both are equally immoral," observed one of the guests, "for they both have the same object - to take away life. The State is not God. It has not the right to take away what it cannot restore when it wants to."

Among the guests was a young lawyer, a young man of five-and-twenty. When he was asked his opinion, he said:

"The death sentence and the life sentence are equally immoral, but if I had to choose between the death penalty and imprisonment for life, I would certainly choose the second. To live anyhow is better than not at all."

A lively discussion arose. The banker, who was younger and more nervous in those days, was suddenly carried away by excitement; he struck the table with his fist and shouted at the young man:

"It's not true! I'll bet you two million you wouldn't stay in solitary confinement for five years."

"If you mean that in earnest," said the young man, "I'll take the bet, but I would stay not five but fifteen years."

2.

"Fifteen? Done!" cried the banker. "Gentlemen, I stake two million!"

"Agreed! You stake your millions and I stake my freedom!" said the young man.

And this wild, senseless bet was carried out! The banker, spoilt and frivolous, with millions beyond his reckoning, was delighted at the bet. At supper he made fun of the young man, and said:

"Think better of it, young man, while there is still time. To me two million is a trifle, but you are losing three or four of the best years of your life. I say three or four, because you won't stay longer. Don't forget either, you unhappy man, that voluntary confinement is a great deal harder to bear than compulsory. The thought that you have the right to step out in liberty at any moment will poison your whole existence in prison. I am sorry for you."

And now the banker, walking to and fro, remembered all this, and asked himself: "What was the object of that bet? What is the good of that man's losing fifteen years of his life and my throwing away two million? Can it prove that the death penalty is better or worse than imprisonment for life? No, no. It was all nonsensical and meaningless. On my part it was the caprice of a pampered man, and on his part simple greed for money ..."

Then he remembered what followed that evening. It was decided that the young man should spend the years of his captivity under the strictest supervision in one of the lodges in the banker's garden. It was agreed that for fifteen years he should not be free to cross the threshold of the lodge, to see human beings, to hear the human voice, or to receive letters and newspapers. He was allowed to have a musical instrument and books, and was allowed to write letters, to drink wine, and to smoke. By the terms of the agreement, the only relations he could have with the outer world were by a little window made purposely for that object. He might have anything he wanted - books, music, wine, and so on - in any quantity he desired by writing an order, but could only receive them through the window. The agreement provided for every detail and every trifle that would make his imprisonment strictly solitary, and bound the young man to stay there exactly fifteen years, beginning from twelve o'clock of November 14, 1870, and ending at twelve o'clock of November 14, 1885. The slightest attempt on his part to break the conditions, if only two minutes before the end, released the banker from the obligation to pay him the two million.

3.

For the first year of his confinement, as far as one could judge from his brief notes, the prisoner suffered severely from loneliness and depression. The sounds of the piano could be heard continually day and night from his lodge. He refused wine and tobacco. Wine, he wrote, excites the desires, and desires are the worst foes of the prisoner; and besides, nothing could be more dreary than drinking good wine and seeing no one. And tobacco spoilt the air of his room. In the first year the books he sent for were principally of a light character; novels with a complicated love plot, sensational and fantastic stories, and so on.

In the second year the piano was silent in the lodge, and the prisoner asked only for the classics. In the fifth year music was audible again, and the prisoner asked for wine. Those who watched him through the window said that all that year he spent doing nothing but eating and drinking and lying on his bed, frequently yawning and angrily talking to himself. He did not read books. Sometimes at night he would sit down to write; he would spend hours writing, and in the morning tear up all that he had written. More than once he could be heard crying.

In the second half of the sixth year the prisoner began zealously studying languages, philosophy, and history. He threw himself eagerly into these studies - so much so that the banker had enough to do to get him the books he ordered. In the course of four years some six hundred volumes were procured at his request. It was during this period that the banker received the following letter from his prisoner:

"My dear Jailer, I write you these lines in six languages. Show them to people who know the languages. Let them read them. If they find not one mistake I implore you to fire a shot in the garden. That shot will show me that my efforts have not been thrown away. The geniuses of all ages and of all lands speak different languages, but the same flame burns in them all. Oh, if you only knew what unearthly happiness my soul feels now from being able to understand them!" The prisoner's desire was fulfilled. The banker ordered two shots to be fired in the garden.

4.

Then after the tenth year, the prisoner sat immovably at the table and read nothing but the Gospel. It seemed strange to the banker that a man who in four years had mastered six hundred learned volumes should waste nearly a year over one thin book easy of comprehension. Theology and histories of religion followed the Gospels.

In the last two years of his confinement the prisoner read an immense quantity of books quite indiscriminately. At one time he was busy with the natural sciences, then he would ask for Byron or Shakespeare. There were notes in which he demanded at the same time books on chemistry, and a manual of medicine, and a novel, and some treatise on philosophy or theology. His reading suggested a man swimming in the sea among the wreckage of his ship, and trying to save his life by greedily clutching first at one spar and then at another.

The old banker remembered all this, and thought:

"To-morrow at twelve o'clock he will regain his freedom. By our agreement I ought to pay him two million. If I do pay him, it is all over with me: I shall be utterly ruined."

Fifteen years before, his millions had been beyond his reckoning; now he was afraid to ask himself which were greater, his debts or his assets. Desperate gambling on the Stock Exchange, wild speculation and the excitability whic h he could not get over even in advancing years, had by degrees led to the decline of his fortune and the proud, fearless, self-confident millionaire had become a banker of middling rank, trembling at every rise and fall in his investments. "Cursed bet!" muttered the old man, clutching his head in despair "Why didn't the man die? He is only forty now. He will take my last penny from me, he will marry, will enjoy life, will gamble on the Exchange; while I shall look at him with envy like a beggar, and hear from him every day the same sentence: 'I am indebted to you for the happiness of my life, let me help you!' No, it is too much! The one means of being saved from bankruptcy and disgrace is the death of that man!"

5.

It struck three o'clock, the banker listened; everyone was asleep in the house and nothing could be heard outside but the rustling of the chilled trees. Trying to make no noise, he took from a fireproof safe the key of the door which had not been opened for fifteen years, put on his overcoat, and went out of the house.

It was dark and cold in the garden. Rain was falling. A damp cutting wind was racing about the garden, howling and giving the trees no rest. The banker strained his eyes, but could see neither the earth nor the white statues, nor the lodge, nor the trees. Going to the spot where the lodge stood, he twice called the watchman. No answer followed. Evidently the watchman had sought shelter from the weather, and was now asleep somewhere either in the kitchen or in the greenhouse.

"If I had the pluck to carry out my intention," thought the old man, "Suspicion would fall first upon the watchman."

He felt in the darkness for the steps and the door, and went into the entry of the lodge. Then he groped his way into a little passage and lighted a match. There was not a soul there. There was a bedstead with no bedding on it, and in the corner there was a dark cast-iron stove. The seals on the door leading to the prisoner's rooms were intact.

When the match went out the old man, trembling with emotion, peeped through the little window. A candle was burning dimly in the prisoner's room. He was sitting at the table. Nothing could be seen but his back, the hair on his head, and his hands. Open books were lying on the table, on the two easy-chairs, and on the carpet near the table.

Five minutes passed and the prisoner did not once stir. Fifteen years' imprisonment had taught him to sit still. The banker tapped at the window with his finger, and the prisoner made no movement whatever in response. Then the banker cautiously broke the seals off the door and put the key in the keyhole. The rusty lock gave a grating sound and the door creaked. The banker expected to hear at once footsteps and a cry of astonishment, but three minutes passed and it was as quiet as ever in the room. He made up his mind to go in.

6.

At the table a man unlike ordinary people was sitting motionless. He was a skeleton with the skin drawn tight over his bones, with long curls like a woman's and a shaggy beard. His face was yellow with an earthy tint in it, his cheeks were hollow, his back long and narrow, and the hand on which his shaggy head was propped was so thin and delicate that it was dreadful to look at it. His hair was already streaked with silver, and seeing his emaciated, aged-looking face, no one would have believed that he was only forty. He was asleep ... In front of his bowed head there lay on the table a sheet of paper on which there was something written in fine handwriting.

"Poor creature!" thought the banker, "he is asleep and most likely dreaming of the millions. And I have only to take this half-dead man, throw him on the bed, stifle him a little with the pillow, and the most conscientious expert would find no sign of a violent death. But let us first read what he has written here ... "

The banker took the page from the table and read as follows:

"To-morrow at twelve o'clock I regain my freedom and the right to associate with other men, but before I leave this room and see the sunshine, I think it necessary to say a few words to you. With a clear conscience I tell you, as before God, who beholds me, that I despise freedom and life and health, and all that in your books is called the good things of the world.

"For fifteen years I have been intently studying earthly life. It is true I have not seen the earth nor men, but in your books I have drunk fragrant wine, I have sung songs, I have hunted stags and wild boars in the forests, have loved women ... Beauties as ethereal as clouds, created by the magic of your poets and geniuses, have visited me at night, and have whispered in my ears wonderful tales that have set my brain in a whirl. In your books I have climbed to the peaks of Elburz and Mont Blanc, and from there I have seen the sun rise and have watched it at evening flood the sky, the ocean, and the mountain-tops with gold and crimson. I have watched from there the lightning flashing over my head and cleaving the storm-clouds. I have seen green forests, fields, rivers, lakes, towns. I have heard the singing of the sirens, and the strains of the shepherds' pipes; I have touched the wings of comely devils who flew down to converse with me of God ... In your books I have flung myself into the bottomless pit, performed miracles, slain, burned towns, preached new religions, conquered whole kingdoms ...

7.

"Your books have given me wisdom. All that the unresting thought of man has created in the ages is compressed into a small compass in my brain. I know that I am wiser than all of you.

"And I despise your books, I despise wisdom and the blessings of this world. It is all worthless, fleeting, illusory, and deceptive, like a mirage. You may be proud, wise, and fine, but death will wipe you off the face of the earth as though you were no more than mice burrowing under the floor, and your posterity, your history, your immortal geniuses will burn or freeze together with the earthly globe.

"You have lost your reason and taken the wrong path. You have taken lies for truth, and hideousness for beauty. You would marvel if, owing to strange events of some sorts, frogs and lizards suddenly grew on apple and orange trees instead of fruit, or if roses began to smell like a sweating horse; so I marvel at you who exchange heaven for earth. I don't want to understand you.

"To prove to you in action how I despise all that you live by, I renounce the two million of which I once dreamed as of paradise and which now I despise. To deprive myself of the right to the money I shall go out from here five hours before the time fixed, and so break the compact ..."

When the banker had read this he laid the page on the table, kissed the strange man on the head, and went out of the lodge, weeping. At no other time, even when he had lost heavily on the Stock Exchange, had he felt so great a contempt for himself. When he got home he lay on his bed, but his tears and emotion kept him for hours from sleeping.

Next morning the watchmen ran in with pale faces, and told him they had seen the man who lived in the lodge climb out of the window into the garden, go to the gate, and disappear. The banker went at once with the servants to the lodge and made sure of the flight of his prisoner. To avoid arousing unnecessary talk, he took from the table the writing in which the millions were renounced, and when he got home locked it up in the fireproof safe.

The Bet Summary

Anton Chekov's "The Bet" is a powerful short story published in 1889 about a banker and a lawyer who make a bet with each other about the death penalty versus life in prison. In the story, each wrestles with the idea of which is better or worse, and the culmination is a twist ending.

The story opens with the banker remembering a bet he made nearly fifteen years earlier with a lawyer. The two fell into a discussion during a party he was hosting and began to debate whether life in prison or death would be more humane. For the banker, capital punishment would be the preferable choice. The lawyer swore he would choose life in prison. They agreed on a bet of two million rubles to see if the lawyer could spend fifteen years in solitary confinement; the lawyer put himself into isolation.

From here, we begin to see the transformation of the lawyer. At first, he suffers. He is depressed and severely lonely. This state, however, gives way to a period of great learning and self-reflection. We see him studying vigorously, first languages, then science, and then a host of other philosophical subjects. Overall, he reads more than 600 volumes in the span of four years. After that, he spends his time studying the Gospels and other histories of religion. In the last two years of his isolation, he returns to the sciences and philosophy.

While this is happening, the banker's fortune declines. He realizes towards the end of the lawyer's confinement that he will be unable to pay the bet if the lawyer triumphs and this debt will completely ruin him. He makes a desperate plan to kill the lawyer so he will not have to pay the debt.

However, on his way to carry out his plan, he finds a note written by the lawyer. In the note, the lawyer explains that his time in isolation has changed him, and he believes that it is best to renounce his wealth and live simply. Material goods are fleeting, and he now despises them in favor of knowledge. Because of his newfound belief, he wishes to renounce the bet.

The banker is moved and leaves the lodge weeping. He is relieved that he does not have to carry out his plan. Although the lawyer technically won the bet by proving he could survive fifteen years of solitary confinement, he also loses the bet by renouncing it.

This story touches on the idea that confinement can fundamentally change who a person is. In death, there is no chance for this great change, but confinement might give a person a chance to have a transformation of character. The lawyer begins his journey with the intention of winning a great deal of money, but in the end, his experience leads him to a completely different way of viewing life.

One interesting theme is the idea of experience. The lawyer claims that through his confinement, he was able to read about all manner of human experiences, and he concludes that this is the same as having the experience itself. He's decided to renounce most of these experiences without ever having them directly.

It is a strange transformation and one we don't expect. Chekov leaves it up to the reader to decide if the lawyer has wasted some of the best years of his life, or if he has transformed for the better through his epiphanies about the nature of experience. The clear thing is that this transformation saved his life when the banker changed his mind.

Another fundamental theme of the story is that of life and death. In the original argument, the guests are unsure which would be more humane or more implicitly a worse punishment. Is life worth the price of death if that life is lived in confinement? What is it that makes life good enough to live and is death preferable to life without freedom? Chekov does not definitively answer those questions, and again, it is up to the reader to decide if the lawyer's transformation is preferable to death. The lawyer seems to think so, but ultimately Chekov's intention is unclear.

An implicit theme of the story is that of humanity. In the beginning, both the banker and the lawyer make a critical bet based on money. At the end of fifteen years, the thought of that money has driven the banker to the point of murder. He only changes course when he realizes that he will not owe the money after all.

On the surface, the lawyer seems to experience a transformation of character, but we are unsure if his transformation is a positive one. He has disavowed all human experiences in his isolation, and while material goods no longer hold sway over him, it is likely that the extreme isolation has still robbed him of his humanity. Chekov makes no move to answer that, and it is up to the reader to decide if the sacrifice has been worth it.

Overall, the story is an interesting insight into what desires drive humanity, and what sorts of things we are willing to do for material gain. It also calls into question our relationships with those around us, insinuating that extreme isolation, while possibly a better alternative than death, will cause us to lose our humanity.

Short Question Answer

Q. 1. Why did the banker weep to read the notes of the lawyer ?

Ans. The banker wept to read the notes of the lawyer because he was filled with guilt. He felt contempt for herself.

Q.2. Who were the persons envolved in the bet ?

Ans. The banker, a rich and young person, and the lawyer, a young man, were the persons involved in the bet.

Q.3. Why was the banker afraid of honouring the bet ?

Ans. The lawyer was confined for long period of fifteen years. The bankers was very rich but his economic condition had become weak by the fourteenth-fifteenth year of lawyers confinement. So, he was being afraid of honouring the bet.

Q. 4. Is capital pusnishment justified ?

Ans. No, capital punishment is not justified. If someone is wrong and commits a crime there are so many ways to condemn and punish him. But life of anyone is very precious. If we cannot give it, we should not take it.

Q.5. How did the lawyer violate the agreement with the banker ?

Ans. The lawyer violated the agreement with the banker by escaping from his cell five minutes before the stipulated term. He went to the gate and disappeared. He did not claim two million roubles from the lawyer because he hated material things.

Q. 6. What was the banker's view on capital punishment and life imprisonement ?

Ans. The banker held a different view from others, who at tended the party while discovering capital punishment was more moral and more humane than life imprisonment. Because execution kills instantly, life imprisonment kills by degree.

Q.7. What were the terms and conditions of the bet ? Do you think them proper ?

Ans. The terms and conditions were the lawyer had to remain confined in a cell for fifteen years. During his confinement the banker had to supply the necessary requisites to the lawyer, for example, food, wine, books and the means of entertainment. If the lawyer successfully remained within the confinement the banker had to pay two millions at stake.

I do not think them as proper, Because vain longings and rigidity of opinions often give bad results. Ultimately the involved parties get nothing but remorse. Pleasure of gain and pleasure of loss both are futile if real wisdom is perceived.

Q. 8. What did the banker do to know that the lawyer had escaped ? Why did he weep to read the notes of the lawyer ?

Ans. The banker instantly went with his servants to the wing and established the escape of his prisoner. To avoid unnecessary Remours he took the paper from the table and on his return locked it in his sate. He wept to see the innocence and greatness of the lawyer.

Q.9. Why was the banker afraid of honouring the bet ? Or, Why was the banker afraid of the Lawyer ?

Ans. The banker had a lot of money when he offered to pay the stake. In course of time, his financial condition had worsened. The lawyer was about to complete fifteen years of his confinement. He thought that he would be ruined for ever and the lawyer would enjoy life. He was afraid of honouring the bet because he did not want to become a beggar.

Q.10. What did the banker do to kill the lawyer ?

Ans. At three o'clock in the dark and chilly night, the banker took the key of the cell and approached the garden wing. Then he entered a narrow passage and struck a match. He peeped through the window into the cell of the lawyer. He removed the seals from the door and opened it. Then he entered the cell to kill the lawyer.

Q.11. What had the prisoner written in his note ?

Ans. The lawyer wrote in his note that he had studied earthly life for fifteen years. The books which he had studied during his confinement had given him wisdom. He said that death will wipe everything from the face of the earth. Now he hated the bet money. Therefore, he had decided to violate the agreement by escaping from the cell five minutes before the fixed time.

Q.12.What are the respective positions of the banker and the lawyer with respect to capital punishment?

Ans. The banker believes that the death penalty is more humane than life imprisonment and argues that no one could stand being alone for a long time. The lawyer, on the other hand, argues that the death penalty is more inhumane than life imprisonment because you are depriving someone of their life–something that you cannot give back. Therefore, life imprisonment is preferable because you will still be alive throughout, and there will always remain the chance that will be freed. This philosophical disagreement is what motivates the bet; in fact, the bet itself can be seen as an extension of this very argument.

Q.13. Why does the lawyer extend the bet from 5 to 15 years?

Ans. Initially, the banker makes the bet for 5 years. He believes that the lawyer would not be able to endure 5 years of voluntary imprisonment. In the heat of the moment, the lawyer raises the stakes to fifteen years. He probably does this to prove how serious he is, and how much he believes that he is in the right. This is corroborated by the fact that he ultimately intentionally loses the bet just 5 hours before he would have won it: he makes deliberate choices in an effort to prove his commitment to his principles.

Q.14.Is the narrator impartial? Why or why not?

Ans. No, the narrator imbues his opinion into his statements. When the bet is first made, the narrator calls it a "wild, senseless bet" punctuating his remarks with an exclamation point (7). The narrator is most decidedly not impartial in his descriptions of the lawyer's imprisonment, too, for he describes him with sympathy and empathy. Most deeply, the narrator is not impartial because he sometimes provides us with insights into the thoughts of the banker, which colours the overall narrative accordingly.

Q.15: What does the lawyer do to take solace in his time of imprisonment? How does his attention shift over the course of his imprisonment?

Ans. The lawyer plays the piano, reads a lot of books, and learns several languages. Though he initially shies away from wine and tobacco, he later turns to them for comfort .The piano sits silent after the first year of his imprisonment, however; progressively, the lawyer focuses more on reading and the acquisition of knowledge, up to the point at which he spends an entire year reading the Gospel. Thus we could describe him as starting out focusing on comforts, and transitioning towards a total focus on enlightenment.

Q.16.How does the lawyer decide to conclude the bet, and why?

Ans. At the end of the fifteen years, five hours before he would have gotten the 2 million rubles, the lawyer chooses to run away and revoke his right to the money, leaving a letter explaining himself. He has come to hate people and rejects the money on principle. This is the direct result of the learning he undertook while imprisoned: with his newfound knowledge of the world, material goods, including money, mean nothing to him, and he hates people for confusedly valuing these things so much.

Long Question Answer

Q. 1. Write a short note on the techniques used by Anton Chekov in "The Bet".

Ans. "The Bet" is a short story where the author speaks in the third person. But the thoughts of the main characters are in the first person. It must be noted that Chekhov had at first written stories for monetary gain, but later on, as his artistic faculties matured and his ambition grew, he started experimenting with various techniques which influenced the evolution of the modern short story. His originality consists in early use of the stream of consciousness technique which James Joyce, Virginia Woolf, Dorothy Richardson and others adopted in their writings. Though the basic narrative technique is to use the authorial voice through third-person narrative, there are some moments in the story where workings of the banker's mind are revealed through the technique of stream of consciousness.

In the story, you can sense the mental turmoil in the banker when he questions himself on the object of the bet. "What was the object of the bet? What is the good of that man's losing fifteen years of life and my throwing away two million?" He realises the futility of the "nonsensical" bet. And it is again with revulsion that we perceive the perverted thoughts of the banker when he decides to murder the lawyer. In fact, he even went to the extent of blaming the watchmen for his own deed. "If I had the pluck to carry out my intention', thought the old man, 'suspicion would fall first upon the watchman.'"

Chekhov very beautifully reveals the atmosphere of the mind of the lawyer through the letter that he writes to the banker in which he gave up the two million roubles. The long letter charts his mental condition when he decides to renounce everything by which ordinary people live. Chekhov, in fact, poses a question to his readers in the sense that we are made to think for ourselves about the transience of material happiness. He believes that the role of an artist is to ask questions, and not to answer them. His use of language is direct and he gives no breathing space to the reader. You can feel yourself carried forward by the sheer virtuosity of his literary genius.

We may recall what Dmitry Grigorovich, a celebrated Russian writer of his day, once wrote to Chekhov. He wrote that Chekhov had real talent- a talent which placed him in the front rank among writers in the new generation. He also advised Chekhov to write less and concentrate more on literary quality, an advice which really inspired the young Chekhov. And you can today see how he has evolved into one of the greatest writers of the world. "The Bet" is one of the most memorable short stories in world literature, both for his technical excellence and richness of content. A fundamental truth of human life-triumph of spiritual values over materialistic fulfilment has been conveyed through a starkly simple story and use of vocabulary that makes it easy reading.

After going through this unit, you have gained an idea about the life and works of Anton Chekhov, the great Russian writer. He was a writer with a keen social conscience and his works are noted for their realistic portrayal of men and manners. In this unit, you have read his short story, "The Bet", which is based on a bet laid between two persons- a banker and a lawyer, and the consequences which follow from it. The story upholds the message that material things do not matter in the long run, and how only spiritualism can lead to eternal bliss. The characters of the two protagonists are beautifully drawn and their emotional and mental upheavals are well delineated. The main theme of the story is that of renouncing material happiness. It is beautifully expressed through his narrative. Chekhov had a great influence on the generation of writers following him and he is indeed a rare genius who delights and instructs at the same time.

CHAPTER FIVE

The Blind Dog

By R. K. Narayan

IT was not a very impressive or high-class dog ; it was one of those commonplace dogs one sees everywhere, colour of white and dust, tail mutilated at a young age by God knows whom, born in the street, and bred on the leavings and garbage of the market-place. He had spotty eyes and undistinguished carriage and needless pugnacity. Before he was two years old he had earned the scars of a hundred fights on his body. When he needed rest on hot afternoons he lay curled up under the culvert at the eastern gate of the market. In the evenings he set out on his daily rounds, loafed in the surrounding streets and lanes, engaged himself in skirmishes, picked up edibles on the roadside, and was back at the market gate by nightfall.

This life went on for three years. And then occurred a change in his life. A beggar, blind of both eyes, appeared at the market gate. An old woman led him up there early in the morning, seated him at the gate, and came up again at midday with some food, gathered his coins, and took him home at night.

The dog was sleeping near by. He was stirred by the smell of food. He got up, came out of his shelter, and stood before the blind man, wagging his tail and gazing expectantly at the bowl, as he was eating his sparse meal. The blind man swept his arms about and asked : " Who is there ? " At which the dog went up and licked his hand. The blind man stroked its coat gently tail to ear and said : " What a beauty you are. Come with me " He threw a handful of food which the dog ate gratefully. It was perhaps an auspicious moment for starting a friendship. They met every day there, and the dog cut off much of its rambling to sit up beside the blind man and watch him receive alms morning to evening. In course of time observing him, the dog understood that the passers-by must give a coin, and whoever went away without dropping a coin was chased by the dog ; he tugged the edge of their clothes by his teeth and pulled them back to the old man at the gate and let go only after something was dropped in his bowl.

Among those who frequented this place was a village urchin, who had the mischief of a devil in him. He liked to tease the blind man by calling him names and by trying to pick up the coins in his bowl. The blind man helplessly shouted and cried and whirled his staff. On Thursdays this boy appeared at the gate, carrying on his head a basket loaded with cucumber or plantain. Every Thursday afternoon it was a crisis in the blind man's life. A seller of bright coloured but doubtful perfumes with his wares mounted on a wheeled platform, a man who spread out cheap story-books on a gunny sack, another man who carried coloured ribbons on an elaborate frame these were the people who usually gathered under the same arch, On a Thursday when the young man appeared at the Eastern gate one of them remarked, " Blind fellow ! Here comes your scourge "

"Oh, God, is this Thursday?" he wailed. He swept his arms about and called : " Dog, dog, come here, where are you ? " He made the peculiar noise which brought the dog to his side. He stroked his head and muttered : " Don't let that little rascal "

At this very moment the boy came up with a leer on his face.

" Blind man ! Still pretending you have no eyes. If you are really blind, you should not know this either " He stopped, his hand moving towards the bowl. The dog sprang on him and snapped his jaws on wrist. The boy extricated his hand and ran for his life. The dog bounded up behind him and chased him out of the market.

" See the mongrel's affection for this old fellow!" marvelled the perfume-vendor.

One evening at the usual time the old woman failed to turn up, and the blind man waited at the gate, worrying as the evening grew into night. As he sat fretting there, a neighbour came up and said : " Sami, don't wait for the old woman. She will not come again. She died this afternoon "

The blind man lost the only home he had, and the only person who cared for him in this world. The ribbon-vendor suggested : " Here, take this white tape " He held a length of the white cord which he had been selling " I will give this to you free of cost. Tie it to the dog and let him lead you about if he is really so fond of you "

Life for the dog took a new turn now. He came to take the place of the old woman. He lost his freedom completely. His world came to be circumscribed by the limits of the white cord which the ribbon-vendor had spared. He had to forget wholesale all his old life all his old haunts. He simply had to stay on for ever at the end of that string. When he saw other dogs, friends or foes, instinctively he sprang up, tugging the string, and this invariably earned him a kick from his master. " Rascal, want to tumble me down, have sense " In a few days the dog learnt to discipline his instinct and impulse. He ceased to take notice of other dogs, even if they came up and growled at his side. He lost his own orbit of movement and contact with his fellow-creatures.

To the extent of this loss his master gained. He moved about as he had never moved in his life. All day he was on his legs, led by the dog. With the staff in one hand and the dog-lead in the other he moved out of his home a corner in a choultry veranda a few yards off the market : he had moved in there after the old woman's death. He started out early in the day. He found that he could treble his income by moving about instead of staying in one place. He moved down the choultry street, and wherever he heard people's voices he stopped and held out his hands for alms. Shops, schools, hospitals, hotels he left nothing out. He gave a tug when he wanted the dog to stop, and shouted like a bullock-driver when he wanted him to move on. The dog protected his feet from going into pits, or stumping against steps or stones, and took him up inch by inch on safe ground and steps. For this sight people gave coins and helped him. Children gathered round him and gave him things to eat. A dog is essentially an active creature who punctuates his hectic rounds with well-defined periods of rest. But now this dog (henceforth to be known as Tiger) had lost all rest. He had rest only when the old man sat down somewhere. At night the old man slept with the cord turned around his finger.

"I can't take chances with you," he said. A great desire to earn more money than ever before seized his master, so that he felt any resting a waste of opportunity, and the dog had to be continuously on his feet. Sometimes his legs refused to move. But if he slowed down even slightly his master goaded him on fiercely with his staff. The dog whined and groaned under this thrust. " Don't whine, you rascal. Don't I give you your food ? You want to loaf, do you ? " swore the blind man. The dog lumbered up and down and round and round the market-place on slow steps, tied down to the blind tyrant. Long after the traffic at the market ceased, you could hear the night stabbed by the far-off wail of the tired dog. It lost its original appearance. As months rolled on, bones stuck up at his haunches and ribs were reliefed through his fading coat.

The ribbon-seller, the novel-vendor and the perfumer observed it one evening, when business was slack, and held a conference among themselves : "It rends my heart to see that poor dog slaving. Can't we do something ? " The ribbon-seller remarked : " That rascal has started lending money for interest I heard it from that fruit-seller He is earning more than he needs. He has become a very devil for money "

At this point the perfumer's eyes caught the scissors dangling from the ribbon-rack. "Give it here," he said and moved on with the scissors in hand.

The blind man was passing in front of the Eastern gate. The dog was straining the lead. There was a piece of bone lying on the way and the dog was straining to pick it up. The lead became taut and hurt the blind man's hand, and he tugged the string and kicked till the dog howled. It howled, but could not pass the bone lightly ; it tried to make another dash for it. The blind man was heaping curses on it. The perfumer stepped up, applied the scissors and snipped the cord. The dog bounced off and picked up the bone. The blind man stopped dead where he stood, with the other half of the string dangling in his hand. " Tiger ! Tiger ! Where are you ? " he cried. The perfumer moved away quietly, muttering : "You heartless devil ! You will never get at him again! He has his freedom!" The dog went off at top speed. He nosed about the ditches happily, hurled himself on other dogs, and ran round and round the fountain in the market-square barking, his eyes sparkling with joy. He returned to his favourite haunts and hung about the butcher's shop, tea-stall, and the bakery.

The ribbon-vendor and his two friends stood at the market gate and enjoyed the sight immensely as the blind man struggled to find his way about. He stood rooted to the spot waving his stick ; he felt as if he were hanging in mid-air. He was wailing. "Oh, where is my dog? Where is my dog? Won't someone give him back to me? I will murder it when I get at it again!" He groped about, tried to cross the road, came near being run over by a dozen vehicles at different points, tumbled and struggled and gasped." He'd deserve it if he was run over, this heartless blackguard" they said, observing him. However, the old man struggled through and with the help of someone found his way back to his corner in the choultry veranda and sank down on his gunnysack bed, half faint with the strain of his journey.

He was not seen for ten days, fifteen days and twenty days. Nor was the dog seen anywhere. They commented among themselves. "The dog must be loafing over the whole earth, free and happy. The beggar is perhaps gone for ever" Hardly was this sentence uttered when they heard the familiar tap-tap of the blind man's staff. They saw him again coming up the pavement led by the dog.

"Look! Look!" they cried. "He has again got at it and tied it up." The ribbon-seller could not contain himself. He ran up and said : " Where have you been all these days ? "

"Know what happened!" cried the blind man. "This dog ran away. I should have died in a day or two, confined to my corner, no food, not an anna to earn imprisoned in my corner. I should have perished if it continued for another day. But this thing returned."

"When? When?"

"Last night. At midnight as I slept in bed, he came and licked my face. I felt like murdering him. I gave him a blow which he will never forget again," said the blind man." I forgave him, after all a dog! He loafed as long as he could pick up some rubbish to eat on the road, but real hunger has driven him back to me, but he will not leave me again. See! I have got this" and he shook the lead : it was a steel chain this time.

Once again there was the dead, despairing look in the dog's eyes. "Go on, you fool," cried the blind man, shouting like an ox-driver. He tugged the chain, poked with the stick, and the dog moved away on slow steps. They stood listening to the tap-tap going away.

"Death alone can help that dog," cried the ribbon-seller, looking after it with a sigh. "What can we do with a creature who returns to his doom with such a free heart?"

The Blind Dog SUMMARY

The lesson 'The Blind dog' is a short narrative written by R.K. Narayan. The story is about a faithful street dong and a blind beggar. The writer describes how human beings treat animals and their incompassionate attitude towards animals. R.K. Narayan is an intrepid story-teller and this story narrates the harrowing and inconsiderate attitude of human beings towards animals. Every Living being is bom free but human nature tries, to capture and bind animals for his own selfishness. The tittle of the story can mislead the reader. Here the dog is not the one who is blind but it befriends a 'blind' man. 'Blind' literally means 'to be not able to see' This is what the writer actually wants convey to his readers. The blind beggar could not 'See' that animals like dog's also need freedom to live their own lives. The dog is 'blind' with his faithfulness towards the 'blind beggar'.

It could not 'see'how inconsidrate and incompassionate the blind man was. The dog is blinded by loyalty and the 'blind man' is blinded by his dependence to the dog, when he takes it for granted and treats it like his slave. 'The Blind Dog' illustrates the dilemma of the street dog tom between his own freedom his loyalty to the blind man. impressive or high class dog but one that is common place seen everywhere. Its colour is white and dust. Its tail was mutilated at a young age. It was bom on the streets and grew up feeding on the garbage of the market place. The dog had spotly eyes and an unim pressive body. But he was short-tempered (Pugnacious) His body was scared because of numerous fights with other dogs. He took rest under a culvert in the market during the afternoons. In the evenings he spent his time loitering in the streets and fighting with other dogs and forage for food. He spent his nights at the market. After three years, his life underwent a drastic change. One day while it was sleeping at the market place it was stirred by the smell of food. He saw a blind beggar eating his sparse meal. He approached the man with expectant eyes and the man stroked it gently and threw a handful of food at it. The dog ate the food gratefully and thus their friendship was sealed.

The beggar was looked after by an old woman. After befriending the beggar the dog spent most of its time with the beggar. It defended the beggar from being harassed. A village urchin stole the blind beggar's coins and teased him. This had been going on every Thursday when the boy would come to the Market to sell vegetables. One Thursday when the boy was up to his usual mischief the faithful dog chased the urchin out of the market. The old woman who had been looking after the beggar died and the beggar was left home eddestitute. The ribbon – seller gave the blind beggar a length of ribbon so that he could tie it around the dogs neck and it could lead him about. Now, the dog lost its freedom completely. The blind man depended on the dog and his dependence made him into a merciless slave – driver. The blind man started earning more because he could move about the market place with the dog leading him. It became a slave to its master. The dog protected the blind man from all dangers and the blind man now became wholly dependent on the dog both for making a living and to live.

He was possessive about the dog and even slept with the dog's leash turned around his finger. The dog was virtually imprisoned and binded to the old man. If the dog grew tired of walking around leading the blind man, he would goad it on fiercely with this staff. At night people could hear the dog's tired wailing stubbing the night air. Before long the dog appeared to be mere bones and skin – he became very thin The ribbon – seller, novel vendor and the perfumer observed the condition of the dog and symphatized with it. The blind-man was now earning more than he required and he started lending money for interest. His greediness grew but the dog grew thinner. One day the perfumer borrowed the scissors from the ribbon vendor and cut of the dog's leash. The dog had regained his freedom. He ran away and happily roamed about the market place. The blind-man was now without any protector he stumbled and grouped about in the market place.

Short Question Answer

Q.1.Why is the story named as the blind dog ?

Ans. The story is titled as "Blind dog" because though the dog was not blind it followed the beggar's orders blindly. A blind person has to be guided by someone else, but here the dog was guided by the blind man. So the title "Blind dog" is a very much accurate title given by the author.

Q.2. What is the moral of the blind dog?

Ans. This story tells us about human greed and cruelty to animals. But the most important message in the story is the loyalty of a dog to his master. The blind beggar treats the dog cruelty. A shopkeeper cute the cord which holds the dog and it becomes free.

Q.3. How the life of both the blind man and the dog change?

Answer: The ribbon seller gave a white cord-free of cost to the blind man. The blind man tied it to the dog and it went wherever the blind man took him. The dog became a prisoner as his world came to be circumscribed by the limits of the white cord.

Q.4. What did the beggar do with the dog?

Ans. The beggar took pity on the old dog. He gave it food and took it with him. The next day, as the beggar and the dog walk around to beg for food and money, they saw a floating basket on the river.

Q.5. How did the dog befriend the blind beggar?

Ans. He saw a blind beggar eating his sparse meal. He approached the man with expectant eyes and the man stroked it gently and threw a handful of food at it. The dog ate the food gratefully and thus their friendship was sealed. ... After befriending the beggar the dog spent most of its time with the beggar.

Q.6. How do you take care of a blind dog?

Ans. For dogs who have lost their sight, maintaining routines as much as possible can help them adjust. Keep your furniture in the same spots to make it easier for your dog to navigate your home. If you redecorate, or when you bring your dog to a new place, bring them carefully around the area to show them obstructions.

Q.7. Why did the beggar weep bitterly that night?

Ans. At the end of the day the poet beggar returned home and emptied his bag on the floor. The poet bitterly wept because he gave the king of kings only a little grain of corn. He realized that if he gave him his all, he would receive much more.

Q.8. How did the dog chase the boy out of the market?

Ans. The boy usually came to pick up the coins in the blind man's bowl. When the old man shouted, the dog came running sprang on him and snapped his jaws on the wrist, the boy extricated his hand and ran for his life. The dog bounded up behind him and chased him out of the market.

Q.9. What is the moral of the blind dog?

Ans. This story tells us about human greed and cruelty to animals. But the most important message in the story is the loyalty of a dog to his master. The blind beggar treats the dog cruelty. A shopkeeper cute the cord which holds the dog and it becomes free.

Long Type Question Answer

Q1. What happened to the dog once it became the blind man's companion?

Ans. The dog started sitting near the old beggar. The old blind beggar used to feed the dog. So it became his companion.

In the beginning, all was well. But the dog's misery started when a ribbon vendor tied a string to it to help the blind man. After that, he held the string of the dog tightly. He started walking with the help of the dog by keeping the string in his hand. Thus more coins started falling into the bowl. It made the person greedier than before. He kept walking throughout the day. The dog's freedom was lost. It became the old man's slave now.

Or

The old blind beggar used to feed the dog. So it became his companion. It started sitting near him. In turn, the dog also started doing favours to the old man. It forced people to drop coins into his bowl. One day, a piece of ribbon attached with a string was tied around its neck. It helped the blind man a lot. Now the dog was not free to run away. It had to remain with him. Thus the dog had to become the old beggar's slave.

Q2. How did the friendship between the dog and the blind man begin?

Ans. one day, the blind beggar was just about to begin eating his food. All of a sudden, he sensed that a dog was sitting near him. So he gave him a small portion of his food to the dog. It continued for some days more and the dog started remaining in the company of the blind man. Thus a friendship started growing between them.

Q3. How did the dog guard the blind man from the urchin?

Ans. On every Thursday, a mischievous boy would come there to sell a load of cucumber or plantain (a vegetable) on his head. He used to tease the beggar by calling him names and picking his coins stealthily. One day, the old man called the dog to save him. The boy tried to pick up coins from the bowl. But the dog noticed this and caught the boy's wrist at once in its mouth. With a great difficulty, the boy freed his wrist and ran away to save himself from the dog.

Q4. Write the character sketch of the blind man.

Ans. The blind man was a greedy person. He was also ungrateful to the dog. He gave the dog just a little portion of his food. But he kept the dog engaged for himself all the time. He did not let the dog enjoy its freedom. He also used to treat the dog harshly. The old man's greed for coins increased day after day. So the troubles of the dog increased. It had to walk with the old man for more time to reach different places. Thus the old blind beggar is not a good human being. He has no sympathy for animals.

Q5. How did the dog's life change after the death of the old woman?

Ans. But after the death of the old woman, the dog's life changed completely. He had to remain all the time with the old man. Now his movements were controlled by the old blind man. So the dog was unable to move to the places of his choice. Sometimes he saw other dogs and wanted to join them. As he tried to pull the string from the old man's hand, it always received (got) a kick from him. Within a few days, the dog had to make a compromise with his changed circumstances (situation), in which he lost all his freedom.

Q6. Describe the life of the dog led after being set free from the blind man.

Ans. One day, a perfume seller took pity on the miserable condition of the dog. So he took a pair of scissors and cut the dog's string. It made him free. The dog ran at his full speed. He visited his favourite places and did activities like smelling about the ditches, sitting in front of the butcher's shop, the tea-stall and the bakery. He would throw himself upon other dogs in a playful mood. He would also run round and round the fountain in the market square barking. His eyes had a special sparkle (shine) of joy in his eyes while doing all these activities.

Q7. What is your opinion about the dog's behaviour?

Ans. The dog's behaviour has two aspects. It is normal before it was free and after it got freedom when his string was cut off by the perfume seller.

After the death of the old woman and when he was tied with a string, his behaviour was a forced one. It was hunger that forced the dog to remain in the company of the blind man.

In the beginning, it sat with the old man because he used to feed him. Later, when he was tied to a string, then also he had to remain with the old man under compulsion. But after some time, the dog was set free as the string was cut by the perfume seller. He enjoyed freedom and went to the places of his choice. That was also his natural behaviour. The dog had to run from one place to the other for food. It was difficult for him to continue with that struggle because he had now another option of getting food from the old blind beggar. So he returns to his old master in the end. This was also the dog's forced behaviour. He was compelled to accept the old man's slavery due to the pangs of hunger.

Q8. Describe the irony contained in the very title of the story 'The Blind Dog'.

Ans. The writer, R. K. Narayana has appropriately titled this story as 'The Blind dog'. It is a great irony that the dog is not blind at all. He can see things quite clearly. It is the old man, who is blind and unable to see the physical world.

The dog joined the blind man's company of his own choice because the old man gave him some food to eat. But after some time, a string was tied to the dog's neck. It made his life miserable. The dog lost all his freedom. Previously, he was free. But now, he lost his freedom.

But when the dog was set free by the perfume seller, he regained his freedom.

But after some time, he again came back to his old master to lose his freedom once again. Herein lies the dog's blindness. The dog accepted the blind man's slavery and this is quite ironic.

<u>Very- Long Answer-type Questions</u>

Q1. Describe the dog of the story. How did it become the blind beggar's companion?

Ans. The dog's story is very interesting and also full of some dramatic turns (changes). He was a mongrel (mixed breed) dog and was born in a street. He had spotty eyes and his hairy coat was of a white and dusty colour. He had a mutilated (cut) tail also.

He could be found taking rest in the hot afternoons under the culvert (a drainage pipe) at the eastern gate of the market. In the evenings, he would start his daily rounds in the surrounding streets to pick up food to satisfy his hunger. But during such wanderings, he had to engage himself in skirmishes (small fights). He would come back to his usual place before nightfall.

The narrator says that it continued for three years and the dog's life changed when a blind beggar began to sit there in the marketplace. An old woman used to lead him up there in the early morning to make him sit there. She would again come up at midday with some foodstuff, collect his coins and take him home at night.

Gradually (slowly), the dog started sitting beside the blind beggar. He would eat food given to him and watch him receive alms from morning to evening.

In the course of time, the dog understood that it was mandatory for the passers-by to drop coins in front of the blind beggar. If the people didn't drop a coin, the dog would chase them, tug at the end of their dress, and pull them back to the beggar to force them to drop a coin or so in the beggar's bowl.

Life went on smoothly for the dog till the old woman, who used to bring food for the blind beggar, lived. After that, the dog's life became miserable.

Q2. What happens to the blind man and the dog at the end of the story?

Ans. At the end of the story, the dog returns to his master, the blind beggar. The dog had become dependent on him for food and shelter. He willingly accepted the old man's slavery. So we may guess that he would never leave the blind beggar.

It means that prosperity would again come in the old man's life. He would do the same type of behaviour with the dog as it was done before. The old man would push the dog with his stick and force him to move forward. More coins would fall into his bowl. He would again start giving money to people on interest. Thus the condition of the dog would be the same. Food again forced the dog to fall in a virtual hell created by the old man.

Q3. How did the life of the blind beggar change when the dog was tied to a string?

Ans. In a way, a turning point came in the life of both, the blind man and the dog too when the tiger (the dog) was tied to a string.

The blind man started moving from one place to the other with the help of the dog.

He used to have his staff (stick) in one hand and the ribbon in the other while moving from one place to the other.

He moved down the 'choultry' (an inn, a resting place) street. He stepped wherever he heard some voice or sensed people's presence. Then he would spread his hand for alms. He went to all the common places like shops, schools, hospitals, hostels, etc.

The dog protected (saved) him from falling into pits or stamping against the stone steps. People started helping him by giving him coins. Children also used to gather around him and give him things to eat.

As time passed, the desire to collect more money grew in the blind man's mind. So he thought taking rest was just a waste of opportunities of collecting money.

CHAPTER SIX

The Child

By PREMCHAND

People call GANGU a brahmin; and GANGU behaves like one. My syce and servants salaam me from a distance. GANGU never does that. Perhaps he expects me to touch his feet. He never handles the tumbler in which I have drunk, and I have never dared to ask him to fan me. Whenever I get drenched in sweat and no one is around, GANGU picks up the fan by himself. But it becomes clear from his looks that he is doing me a favour. And I don't know why I at once snatch the fan from his hands. He is short-tempered and can't stand any criticism. He hardly has my friends. Perhaps he thinks it below his dignity to sit beside my syce and servants. I have never seen him socializing with anyone. What surprises me most is that he is not addicted to bhang or things like that, a habit that is a special characteristic of the people of his caste. I have never seen him performing any religious rituals or bathing in a river. He is totally illiterate; even then he is a Brahmin; and expects others to reverence and serve him. But why shouldn't he? When people are holding onto the wealth inherited from their ancestors under the belief that they themselves have created that wealth, then why should he give up the Village and status bequeathed to him by his ancestors? This is his birth right.

By nature I am reserved with my servants. I don't like them to come to me unless I ask for them. I don't like to shout for them for small matters. I find it more convenient to pour water from the surahi with my own hands, or light the lamp, or put on my shoes, or to take out a book from the shelf, all by myself, than ask Hingan or Maikoo to do any of that. This gives me a feeling of self-reliance and self-confidence. My servants too have understood my nature, and seldom come to me unless I call them. Therefore, one morning when Gangu came and stood in front of me, I didn't like it. These people come to me either to ask for an advance or to complain about one of their companions. And I dislike this. I pay everyone on the first of the month and whenever someone comes to ask for an advance I get worked up. I don't like keeping account of small amounts. And then if someone has got his full wages for a month he has no business to fritter it away in fifteen days and then come and ask for an advance or a loan. And I hate listening to complaints. I look upon them as a sign of weakness or a mean attempt at flattery.

I knitted my brows and said, 'What's the matter? I didn't call you.'

I was amazed to see a look of politeness, supplication and even unease on his proud face. It seemed he wanted to say something but was unable to find words for it.

In irritation I said, 'What's wrong? Why don't you say something? You know it's time for me to go for a walk. I'm getting late.'

Gangu replied in a dejected tone, 'All right, you go for your walk. I'll come again.'

This was still more worrisome. Now, knowing that I don't have much time he would quickly blurt out all in one outburst. On another occasion the rogue would go on bemoaning for hours. He may be regarding my reading and writing as some kind of work, but my moments of contemplation, the most crucial ones of my vocation, are mere relaxation in his eyes. And he would catch hold of me at such a time.

'Have you come to ask for an advance? I don't give advances.' I said, rudely.

'No, sarkar. I have never asked for an advance.'

'Then, have you come to complain against someone? I don't like to listen to complaints.'

'No, sarkar. I have never complained against anyone.'

Gangu now looked determined. From the expression on his face it seemed he was marshaling all his strength for a long hop. He spoke in an unsteady voice, 'Please, relieve me of my duties. Now I won't be able to serve under you.'

I had never before heard this kind of demand. It hurt my self-pride. I consider myself a model of humane behaviour. I don't speak harshly to my servants and try to keep my bossy attitude sheathed in a scabbard. So I was amazed at this plea.

I said in a harsh tone, 'Why? What's your resentment?'

'Very few are as good-natured as you, hazoor, but I'm in a situation in which I can no longer work with you. While I'm here something might happen to bring a bad name to you. I don't want that your reputation should suffer because of me.'

I was perplexed and became inflamed with curiosity. I threw myself into the chair lying in the verandah and said, 'Why do you talk in riddles? Tell me straight what the matter is.'

Very politely Gangu said, 'The truth is that the woman who has been expelled from the Widows' Ashram, the same Gomti Devi...'

I asked impatiently, 'Yes, she has been expelled. So what? What has that to do with your job?'

It was as if Gangu had unloaded a heavy burden from his head, 'I want to marry her, babuji.'

I looked at him with astonishment. This illiterate and orthodox brahmin, untouched by new ideas, is going to marry this shameless whore, whom no one would even let into their house! Gomti had created a stir in the peaceful atmosphere of the mohalla. She had come to this Widows' Ashram a few years ago. The officials of the Ashram had married her off three times, and each time she had left her husband and returned after a few weeks or a month. So much so that the secretary of the Ashram had this time expelled her, and now she lived in a small room in the mohalla and had become a source of fun for the mohalla's bad charcters.

I was angered at Gangu's simplicity but I also pitied him. The donkey could not find any other woman except this one to marry. When she had forsaken three men how long would she stay with him? Had he been a man of money, she might have stayed with him for six months or a year. He is stark blind. She won't stay with him even for a week.

I asked him in a tone of clear warning, 'Don't you know the stories of her misdeeds?'

Gangu spoke as if he had been an eyewitness, 'These are all lies. People have maligned her for nothing.'

'What do you mean? Hasn't she left three men?'

'They drove her out. What could she do?'

'You fool! Does anyone come from so far, spend thousands of rupees just to drive away a woman?'

Gangu, charged with emotion, replied, 'Hazoor, no woman can stay where there's no love. A woman doesn't need just food and clothing. She needs love too. They must have thought they had done a widow a great favour by marrying her. They must have expected her to surrender to them body and soul; but to do that one has first to surrender oneself, hazoor.

That's it. Moreover, she is suffering from a sickness. She is sometimes possessed by a spirit. Then she starts talking nonsense, and falls unconscious.'

'And you'll marry such a woman?' I asked, shaking my head in disbelief. 'Take it from me, you will reap a bitter harvest.'

Gangu shook his head like a martyr and said,' Babuji, I believe it will end happily for me, God willing.'

'Then you have decided finally?' I asked him firmly.

'Yes, hazoor.'

'Then I accept your resignation.'

I am not a prisoner of worn-out customs and orthodoxies, but to keep in my employment a man who was marrying a slut was really a risky proposition. Every now and then there would arise new complications and troubles; the police would come, and court cases. There might even be thefts. So it was advisable to keep off these quicksands. Gangu, like a man hungry from deprivation, is leaping for a piece of bread unmindful that it is a leftover, is dry and unfit to eat. I thought it right to keep him out.

Five months went by. Gangu had married Gomti and he lived in a tiled-roof shack in the same mohalla. Now he made his living by hawking chaat. Whenever I met him in the bazaar, I would enquire about his well-being, for I had become deeply interested in him. His life was a testing ground for a social question, not only social a psychological one too. I was curious to know how this would end. I always found Gangu in a happy state of mind. I could clearly see on his face the sparkle and self-confidence that is the result of happiness and contentment in life. His sale was no more than a rupee and a half, and out of this his earnings came to about eight-to-ten annas. This was his livelihood but it seemed blessed by a god because there was not a trace of the shame and misfortune that is found among such people. On his face there was a look of self-assurance and joy that comes only to a contented soul.

One day I heard that Gomti had deserted Gangu and run away. I don't know why but I derived a strange pleasure from this news. I had become envious of Gangu's happy and contented life, and was waiting for some unhappy, disastrous or shameful end to it. This news gratified my envy. After all the very thing I had expected had happened. The fellow was punished for his lack of foresight. Let me see how he shows his face to me. Now he would realize how right they were who had advised him against this marriage. He had thought that he had come to possess something rare, as if the doors to salvation had opened for him. People had warned him that that woman could not be trusted, that she had deceived so many, but it had all fallen on deaf ears. Now when he meets me I shall ask him how happy he was after this boon from his goddess! He used to say she was this and she was that and people defamed her out of ill will, and now let me see who was mistaken.

The same day I happened to meet Gangu in the market. He was shaken and unsettled, completely lost to himself. Tears welled up in his eyes the moment he saw me, not out of shame but pain. 'Babuji, Gomti deceived me too.' Hiding my malicious pleasure under an outward show of sympathy, I said, 'I had warned you of this and you did not listen. Now have patience. There is nothing else you can do. Has she cleaned you out or left something behind?'

Gangu touched his heart with his hands. It seemed my speech had hurt him deeply.

'Oh babuji, don't say this. She took away nothing. In fact she left behind whatever she had. I don't know what my fault was. May be I was not good enough for her. She was literate and I unlettered. It was enough that she stayed with me for so long. Had she stayed with me a little longer I would have become a good person. What should I tell you about her? I don't know what she was for others but for me she was like a god's blessing. I don't know where I had faulted. I swear I never saw a trace of resentment on her face. I'm nobody, babuji. I earn no more than ten-twelve annas, but she was so good at housekeeping that I never felt the shortage of anything.'

I was acutely disappointed at what he said. I had thought he would narrate the story of her infidelity and I would show my sympathy for him, but his eyes were not yet opened, the fool that he was. He was still under her spell and had become disorientated.

I began to ridicule him, 'So she hasn't carried anything with her.?'

'Nothing at all, babuji. Not a pie.'

'And she loved you very much?'

'How should I convince you, babuji? That love I shall not forget till my death.'

'And even then she deserted you?'

'That's what surprises me, babuji.'

'Haven't you heard the stories of female treachery?'

'Don't say that, babuji. I would keep singing her praises even if someone should threaten to slit my throat.'

'Then go and search for her.'

'Yes, master. I won't rest till I have found her. Once I come to know where she is I shall definitely bring her back, and my heart tells me she will come back. You'll see. She hasn't gone away out of any resentment. I shall search for her everywhere. And when I have found her I'll see you again.'

Saying this he went his way, distraught with emotion.

Just after this meeting I had to go to Nainital for some work and returned after a month. I hadn't yet changed my dress when I saw Gangu standing in front of me holding a newly born baby in his hands. Perhaps even Nand himself would not have been so overjoyed to hold the child Krishna in his lap. Gangu's whole body seemed to exude an uncontrollable joy. His face and eyes were singing with gratitude and love. He displayed the same kind of contentment that one finds on the face of a starving beggar after he had had his fill.

I said, 'Tell me, great man, did you get some news of Gomti Devi? you had gone away to trace her.'

Gangu burst out, 'Yes, babuji. With your blessings I have brought her back. She was found in a hospital in Lucknow. She had confided her whereabouts to one of her female friends here. The moment I came to know I rushed to Lucknow and dragged her back. And I got this baby, over and above.'

He lifted the baby and brought it in full view of me like a sportsman proudly displaying his medal.

I remarked mockingly, 'Very fine, you got this boy, too. Perhaps that is why she had run away. Is he your son?'

'Why mine, babuji? He's yours. God's.'

'Was he born in Lucknow?'

'Yes, babuji, He's just a month old.'

'How long have you been married?'

'This is the seventh month.'

'So he was born in the sixth month of your marriage?'

'What else.'

'And even then he's yours?'

'Yes.'

'You're talking nonsense.'

I am not sure whether he understood what I was trying to say but he replied out of plain innocence, 'Babuji, she nearly died giving him birth. She has got a new life. She struggled between life and death for three days and three nights.'

I taunted him. 'This is the first time I hear that a baby can be born after six months of marriage.'

The arrow had hit the target.

He smiled and said, 'Oh, it's that. I didn't even think of it. That's why Gomti had run away.'

He continued: 'I said "Gomti, if you don't like me, you can leave me. I shall go away and never trouble you again. If you ever need my help, write to me and I shall do everything I can. I have no resentment against you. In my eyes you are still as good as you were before. I love you as before. No, now I love you even more. And if you have not turned away from me, then come with me. Gangu would never be unfaithful to you. I married you not because you are a goddess but because I loved you and believed you also loved me. This child is my child, my own child. I took a sown field. Should I then disown the harvest just because someone else had sown it?" '

Saying this, Gangu burst out into a loud laughter.

I forgot to change my dress. I don't know why but my eyes were filled with tears. I don't know the power that crushed my revulsion and made me open my arms. I took that immaculate child in my lap and kissed his face with the affection that perhaps I had not shown even for my own children.

Gangu said, 'Babuji, you're such a good human being. I have always sung your praises before Gomti. I keep telling her to come and meet you, but she doesn't come out of shyness.'

I a good human being! The veneer of goodness was gone today. I spoke to him with a heart full of devotion, 'No. Why should she come to meet a black-hearted person like me? Come, take me to meet her. You say I'm a good person! No. I'm good only from outside but very mean from inside. It is you who is truly good, and this baby is a flower that radiates the fragrance of your goodness.'

I embraced the baby and walked along side Gangu.

The Child SUMMARY

'The child' is a wonderful story written by PREMCHAND. The story highlights a new sense of social awareness in people.

The story 'The child' is narrated by the narrator who is a generous. GANGU is one of the servants who considers himself as a Brahmin. He is different from many other servants in the household. He is lazy by nature and does not bear the characteristics of an ideal Brahmin. Once he goes to the narrator in private. He hesitates to speak. The narrator thinks that he must have came to either ask for money or to complain about another servant. But the narrator is surprised when GANGU states that he wants to leave the job because he is going to marry a woman named Gomti Devi.

Gomti Devi had been driven away twice by her two past husbands. Now, she has started living in the same MOHALLA. All consider her to be of low character. But GANGU'S opinion is different. The narrator tries to persuade but GANGU does not understand the scenario. Finally he leaves the job. The narrator thinks that very soon Gomati devi and GANGU will get separated but they live happily.

After some time, Gomati runs away. The narrator feels satisfied thinking that he has proved true. GANGU is now upset but still has faith in her. After one month when the narrator returns from Nainital, GANGU comes to see the narrator again. Now, GANGU has found out Gomti with a new born baby. GANGU is not father of that child because Gomti Devi delivers a baby whit in just few months after marriage. The narrator tries hard to provoke him against Gomti about the illegitimacy of the child but he is firm in his love. He accepts the child as a gift from the god. Finally, seeing GANGU'S feeling and generosity, the narrator is touched and offers his blessing to the baby.

Short Question Answer

Q.1. What is the theme of the child by PREMCHAND?

Ans: The child' is a wonderful story written by PREMCHAND. The story highlights a new sense of social awareness in people. The story 'The child' is narrated by the narrator who is a generous.

Q.2. Why did GANGU meet the narrator?

Ans: GANGU wished to meet the narrator and tell him about his wish to be relieved from the duties as his servant. He was not in the position to serve the narrator any longer because he had decided to marry an illreputed woman of the Mohalla. GANGU feared that this act of his would bring illfame for his master.

Q.3. Who was Gomti in the child?

Ans. The story is narrated by his master, who is surprised when Gangu asks to leave his job because he wishes to marry Gomti, a poor woman with two failed marriages behind her. When Gangu and Gomti are married,

Gomti disappears. Gangu eventually finds her again and brings her back with a child, which is not his.

Q.4. How does the child by Premchand treat the question of morality?

Answer: The narrator tried hard to provoke him against Gomati but he was firm in his love. He accepted the child as a gift from the god. Finally, seeing Gangu's feeling and generosity, the narrator was touched and offered his blessing to the baby.

Q.5. How many times had Gomti married before her marriage with Gangu?

Ans. Gangu confesses his love towards a widow named Gomti Devi, and he then marries Gomti, who has betrayed **three husbands** before her marriage with Gangu.

Q.6. How did Gangu find Gomti answer?

Ans. Gangu finds Gomti in her village and she also had a child. The story is about a servant who Brahman by caste but has good manners and kind nature. He married a woman named Gomti who had two failed marriages behind. ... Gomti disappears and Gangu finds him with a child that is not his.

Q.7. How did Gangu fall in love with Gomti?

Ans. One day Gangu confesses his love towards a widow named Gomti Devi, and he also marries Gomti, who has betrayed three husbands before her marriage with Gangu. she realized that she was carrying the baby of her previous husband. Gangu love so much to Gomti he searched it bring her back home from a hospital in Lucknow.

Q.8. Who was Gomti answer?

Ans. Gomti is a poor woman with two failed marriages behind her. When Gangu and Gomti are married, Gomti disappears.

Q.9. Is Gangu's personality different before marriage?

Ans. Gangu remained the same as before the marriage. He was calm and had faith on his wife Gomati devi who already had run away from two husbands that she will come back to him. He was carrying the child as God's gift whose father was someone else.

Q.10. Who is Gangu?

Ans. Gangu was a Brahmin ruler of the Deccan. There is a popular legend regarding him narrated by the 17th century poet Ferishta, which says that Hasan Gangu (Ala-ud-Din Bahman Shah) was a servant of a brahmin ruler named Gangu (hence the name Hasan Gangu), who educated Hasan in Hinduism and made him a general in his army.

Q.11. Why did Gangu approach come to his master day?

Ans. One day, Gangu approaches his master and asks to be relieved of his duties. He's going to marry Gomti, a woman with a notorious reputation. The narrator is aghast; he simply cannot believe that Gangu would actually get married to someone so heartily despised among polite society.

Q.12. Why did Gomti marry Gangu?

Ans. Gangu appears to marry Gomti out of pity. Although Gomti has a bad reputation and has left all her previous husbands, Gangu believes that she was driven out by them and deprived of love.

Q.13. What kind of character does Gomti possess?

Ans. Gomti is more complex. Her failed marriages and illegitimate child suggest to the narrator that she is of low character, but much of the opprobrium she suffers is projected onto her by the restrictive, patriarchal society in which she lives and we hear little from her directly. She remains a mysterious figure.

Q.14. Who convinced the narrator that it was not wrong to marry Gomti?

Answer: The story is narrated by his master, who is surprised when Gangu asks to leave his job because he wishes to marry Gomti, a poor woman with two failed marriages behind her. When Gangu and Gomti are married, Gomti disappears. Gangu eventually finds her again and brings her back with a child, which is not his.

Q.15. Who narrates the story the child?

Ans. 'The child' is a story which is narrated by the narrator who is a generous, rich man. Gangu was one of the servant who served his master. Gangu was a Brahmin. He was different from many other servants in the household.

Long Question Answer

Q.1. How does 'The Child' story by premchand treat the question of morality?

Ans. 'The child' is a beautiful story written by the famous writer Premchand. He brought a new sense of social awareness in people through is novels and short stories. He is respected as an outstanding short story writer.

'The child' is a story which is narrated by the narrator who is a generous, rich man. Gangu was one of the servant who served his master. Gangu was a Brahmin. He was different from many other servants in the household.

He was away from all the vices. Of course he showed no characteristics of an ideal Brahmin. Once he went to the narrator in private. He hesitated to speak. The narrator showed that he was too busy and ordered him to speck quickly. The narrator thought that he must have came to either ask for money or to complain about another servant.

But the narrator was surprised when Gangu declared that he wanted to leave the job because he was going to marry. Gomati Devi who had been driven away twice by her two past husbands. She lived in the same Mohalla and she was respected by name. All believed her to be low in character. But Gangu's opinion was different. The narrator tried to stop but Gangu said that it was not fault. Nobody understood her. Finally he left the job. The narrator thought that very soon Gomati devi and Gangu will get separated but they lived happily.

But once Gomati run away. The narrator was happy thinking that he proved true. Gangu was upset but still had faith in her. After one month when the narrator returned from Nainital, Gangu came to him again. He had a new born baby in his hand. He was extremely happy. He searched and found Gomati out. She had runaway because she was going to be the mother and Gangu was not father of that child. But Gangu was very generous. The narrator tried hard to provoke him against Gomati but he was firm in his love. He accepted the child as a gift from the god.

Finally, seeing Gangu's feeling and generosity, the narrator was touched and offered his blessing to the baby. We are impressed by the courage and sincerely of Gangu here. He proved to be a noble human being.

Q.2. Depiction of Gomti in the story.

Ans. In Munshi Premchand's short story "The Child", Gangu, though a servant, is from the Brahmin caste and is generally regarded as a virtuous and a decent man, superior to other servants in habits as well as class. The story is narrated by his master, who is surprised when Gangu asks to leave his job because he wishes to marry Gomti, a poor woman with two failed marriages behind her.

When Gangu and Gomti are married, Gomti disappears. Gangu eventually finds her again and brings her back with a child, which is not his. However, Gangu forgives her infidelity and sees the child as a gift from God, despite the narrator's attempts to stir him to anger against Gomti.

The character of Gangu is practically the embodiment of goodness and nobility, almost too perfect in his acceptance of Gomti and his forgiveness of her. Throughout the story, he is a paragon of kindness and generosity.

Gomti is more complex. Her failed marriages and illegitimate child suggest to the narrator that she is of low character, but much of the opprobrium she suffers is projected onto her by the restrictive, patriarchal society in which she lives and we hear little from her directly.

Q.3. Character sketch of Gangu in the short story the child ?

Ans. Gangu was a Brahmin servant boy. He was very much different from other servants. He did not bow to his master which shows his character of not doing something just to please people.

Unlike the Brahmans he was not educated, did not take bath in the river or pray regularly.

His broad social mind is exposed in the way he marries Gomti, a widowed women in-spite of people's criticism and resent from his master.

He was not bothered about her past. His pure love for others is revealed when he accepts Gomti with the child of her previous husband.

Thus Gangu is a good man with a kind and generous heart.

CHAPTER SEVEN

The Mark of Vishnu

<u>BY Khushwant Singh</u>

"This is for Kala Nag," said Gunga Ram, pouring the milk into the saucer. "Every night I leave it outside the hole near the wall and it's gone by the morning." "Perhaps it is the cat, "we youngsters suggested.

"Cat!" said Gunga Ram with contempt. "No cat goes near that hole. Kala Nag lives there. As long as I give him milk, he will not bite anyone in this house. You can all go about with bare feet and play where you like."

We were not having any patronage from Gunga Ram.

"You're a stupid old Brahmin," I said. "Don't you know snakes don't drink milk? At least one couldn't drink a saucerful every day. The teacher told us that a snake eats only once in several days. We saw a grass snake which had just swallowed a frog. It stuck like a blob in its throat and took several days to dissolve and go down its tail. We've got dozens of them in the lab, in methylated spirit. Why, last month the teacher bought one from a snake charmer which could run both ways. It had another head with a pair of eyes at the tail. You should have seen the fun when it was put in the jar. There wasn't an empty one in the lab. So the teacher put it in one which had a Russel's viper. He caught its two ends with a pair of forceps, dropped it in the jar, and quickly put the lid on. There was an absolute storm as it went round and round in the glass, tearing the decayed viper into shreds."

Gunga Ram shut his eyes in pious horror.

"You will pay for it one day. Yes, you will."

It was no use arguing with Gunga Ram. He, like all good Hindus, believed in the Trinity of Brahma, Vishnu, and Shiva, the creator, preserver, and destroyer. Of these he was most devoted to Vishnu. Every morning he smeared his forehead with a V mark in sandalwood paste to honour the deity. Although a Brahmin, he was illiterate and full of superstition. To him, all life was sacred, even if it was of a serpent or scorpion or centipede.

Whenever he saw one he quickly shoved it away lest we kill it. He picked up wasps we battered with our badminton rackets and tended their damaged wings. Sometimes he got stung. It never seemed to shake his faith. More dangerous the animal, the more devoted Gunga Ram was to its existence. Hence the regard for snakes; and above all, for the cobra, who was the Kala Nag.

"We will kill your Kala Nag if we see him."

"I won't let you. It's laid a hundred eggs and if you kill it all the eggs will become cobras and the house will be full of them. Then what will you do?"

"We'll catch them alive and send them to Bombay. They milk them there for anti-snakebite serum. They pay two rupees for a live cobra. That makes two hundred rupees straightway."

"Your doctors must have udders. I never saw a snake have any. But don't you dare touch this one. It is a phannyar—it is hooded. I've seen it. It's three hands long. As for its hood!' Gunga Ram opened the palms of his hands and his head swayed from side to side. 'You should see it basking on the lawn in the sunlight."

"That just proves what a liar you are. The phannyar is the male, so it couldn't have laid the hundred eggs. You must have laid the eggs yourself."

The party burst into peals of laughter.

"Must be Gunga Ram's eggs. We'll soon have a hundred Gunga Rams."

Gunga Ram was squashed. It was the lot of a servant to be constantly squashed. But having the children of the household make fun of him was too much even for Gunga Ram .They were constantly belittling him with their new-fangled ideas. They never read their scriptures.

Not even what the Mahatma said about non-violence. It was just shotguns to kill birds and the jars of methylated spirit to drown snakes. Gunga Ram would stick to his faith in the sanctity of life, he would feed and protect snakes because snakes were the most vile of God's creatures on earth. If you could love them, instead of killing them, you proved your point.

What the point was which Gunga Ram wanted to prove was not clear. He just proved it by leaving the saucerful of milk by the snake hole every night and finding it gone in the mornings.

One day we saw Kala Nag. The monsoons had burst with all their fury and it had rained in the night. The earth which had lain parched and dry under the withering heat of the summer sun was teeming with life. In little pools frogs croaked. The muddy ground was littered with crawling worms, centipedes and velvety ladybirds.

Grass had begun to show and the banana leaves glistened bright and glossy green. The rain had flooded Kala Nag's hole. He sat in an open patch on the lawn. His shiny black hood glistened in the sunlight. He was big—almost six feet in length, and rounded and fleshy, like my wrist.

"Looks like a King Cobra. Let's get him."

Kala Nag did not have much of a chance. The ground was slippery and all the holes and gutters were full of water. Gunga Ram was not at home to help.

Armed with long bamboo sticks, we surrounded Kala Nag before he even scented danger. When he saw us his eyes turned a fiery red and he hissed and spat on all sides. Then, like lightning Kala Nag made for the banana grove. The ground was too muddy and he slithered. He had hardly gone five yards when a stick caught him in the middle and broke his back. A volley of blows reduced him to a squishy-squashy pulp of black-and-white jelly, spattered with blood and mud. His head was still undamaged.

"Don't damage the hood," yelled one of us. "We'll take Kala Nag to school."

So we slid a bamboo stick under the cobra's belly and lifted him on the end of the pole. We put him in a large biscuit tin and tied it up with string. We hid the tin under a bed.

At night I hung around Gunga Ram waiting for him to get his saucer of milk. 'Aren't you going to take any milk for Kala Nag tonight?'

"Yes," answered Gunga Ram irritably. "You go to bed."

He did not want any more argument on the subject.

"He won't need the milk any more."

Gunga Ram paused.

"Oh, nothing. There are so many frogs about. They must taste better than your milk. You never put any sugar in it anyway."

The next morning Gunga Ram brought back the saucer with the milk still in it. He looked sullen and suspicious.

"I told you snakes like frogs better than milk."

Whilst we changed and had breakfast Gunga Ram hung around us. The school bus came and we clambered into it with the tin. As the bus started we held out the tin to Gunga Ram.

"Here's your Kala Nag. Safe in this box. We are going to put him in spirit."

We left him standing speechless, staring at the departing bus.

There was great excitement in the school. We were a set of four brothers known for our toughness. We had proved it again.

"A King Cobra."

"Six feet long."

"Phannyar."

The tin was presented to the science teacher.

It was on the teacher's table, and we waited for him to open it and admire our kill. The teacher pretended to be indifferent and set us some problems to work on. With studied matter-of-factness he fetched his forceps and a jar with a banded Krait lying curled in muddy methylated spirit. He began to hum and untie the cord around the box.

As soon as the cord was loosened the lid flew into the air, just missing the teacher's nose. There was Kala Nag. His eyes burnt like embers and his hood was taut and undamaged. With a loud hiss he went for the teacher's face. The teacher pushed himself back on the chair and toppled over. He fell on the floor and stared at the cobra, petrified with fear. The boys stood up on their desks and yelled hysterically.

Kala Nag surveyed the scene with his bloodshot eyes.

His forked tongue darted in and out excitedly. He spat furiously and then made a bid for freedom. He fell out of the tin on to the floor with a loud plop. His back was broken in several places and he dragged himself painfully to the door. When he got to the threshold he drew himself up once again with his hood outspread to face another danger.

Outside the classroom stood Gunga Ram with a saucer and a jug of milk. As soon as he saw Kala Nag come up he went down on his knees. He poured the milk into the saucer and placed it near the threshold. With hands folded in prayer he bowed his head to the ground craving forgiveness. In desperate fury, the cobra hissed and spat and bit Gunga Ram all over the head—then with great effort dragged himself into a gutter and wriggled out of view.

Gunga Ram collapsed with his hands covering his face. He groaned in agony. The poison blinded him instantly. Within a few minutes he turned pale and blue and froth appeared in his mouth. On his forehead were little drops of blood. These the teacher wiped with his handkerchief. Underneath was the V mark where Kala Nag had dug his fangs.

The Mark of Vishnu SUMMARY

In the story, Gunga Ram is a devotee of Vishnu. Vishnu is the preserver and protector of creation. For Gunga Ram, all living things are to be revered and cherished, even dangerous animals.

To him, all life was sacred, even if it was of a serpent or scorpion or centipede.

For the most part, he is an object of derision to the boys in the household. Above all, Gunga Ram's great regard for the Kala Nag (cobra) creates conflict between him and his master's children. It is obvious that Gunga Ram derives a sense of righteous dignity (in his position as a lowly servant) through his devoted defense of such dangerous creatures. Meanwhile, the boys are more concerned about displaying clear evidences of their masculine mastery over such treacherous wild enemies.

In the story, science is pitted against superstition. Both are sorely tested, but science wins in the end. The hapless Gunga Ram is attacked and brutally poisoned by the Kala Nag even as he bows his head in obeisance to the cruel god.

Gunga Ram collapsed with his hands covering his face. He groaned in agony. The poison blinded him instantly. Within a few minutes he turned pale and blue and froth appeared in his mouth. On his forehead were little drops of blood. These the teacher wiped with his handkerchief. Underneath was the V-mark where the Kala Nag had dug his fangs.

In describing the manner of his death, KHUSWANT Singh is highlighting the irony of Gunga Ram's implicit trust in his beliefs. Far from ensuring him long life, his blind worship has caused him to endure a cruel death. Alas, Vishnu, the one god who is supposed to tip the balance of the forces of good and evil in favor of the good, has chosen not to preserve the life of his seemingly devout supplicant, Gunga Ram.

<u>Short Question Answer</u>

Q.1. What is the theme of The Mark of Vishnu?

Ans. The theme of the short story "The Mark of Vishnu" by Khushwant Singh is superstition and ignorance. The main character, Gunga Ram, is both superstitious and ignorant. He believes that by leaving a saucer full of milk for the snake to drink, he is protecting the household from snake bites.

Q.2. Who was Gunga Ram the mark of Vishnu?

Ans. Gunga Ram appears in the short story "The Mark of Vishnu" by Khushwant Singh. He is an old servant and follows the Hindu religion. Although he is a Brahmin, he is uneducated. He worships the Trinity of Brahma, Vishnu, and Siva, in accordance with Hindu beliefs, but he is most devoted to Vishnu.

Q.3. Why is the mark of Vishnu an appropriate title for the story?

Ans : "The Mark of Vishnu" by Khushwant Singh underlines between faith and science. ... Gunga Ram's blind faith and his failure in reasoning the potential threat that a snake possess caused him his death.

Q.4. What is it that Khushwant Singh is trying to convey through his story the mark of Vishnu?

Ans. Basically, Khuswant Singh wants to convey the irony of one's beliefs in The Mark Of Vishnu. In the story, Gunga Ram is a devotee of Vishnu. Vishnu is the preserver and protector of creation. For Gunga Ram, all living things are to be revered and cherished, even dangerous animals.

Q.5. Why Khushwant Singh is famous?

Ans.Khushwant Singh (born Khushal Singh, 2 February 1915 – 20 March 2014) was an Indian author, lawyer, diplomat, journalist and politician. His experience in the 1947 Partition of India inspired him to write Train to Pakistan in 1956 (made into film in 1998), which became his most well-known novel.

Q.6. What does Gunga Ram represent as a person of?

Ans. Gunga Ram becomes the symbol of rigid traditions which do not change under any circumstance. He is fully superstitious and throughout the story is presented as an ignorant man. He represents all the superstitious people especially of the Indian society who did not question the existing beliefs.

Q.7. What part of the Kala Nag remained undamaged?

Ans. His head also remained undamaged. They didn't want the hood to be harmed, so they slipped a bamboo stick under the belly of the cobra and raised it to the end of the pole. They put him in a big tin of biscuits and fastened it with a string, then hid the tin under a bed. That's how kala nag was captured.

Q.8. Which Mark Ganga Ram put on his forehead?

Ans. Every morning he smeared his forehead with a V mark in sandalwood paste to honour the deity. Although a Brahmin, he was illiterate and full of superstition. To him, all life was sacred, even if it was of a serpent or scorpion or centipede. Whenever he saw one he quickly shoved it away lest we kill it.

Q.9. Who is the protagonist of the story the mark of Vishnu?

Ans. The main characters in the short story "The Mark of Vishnu" by Khushwant Singh are Gunga Ram and the four schoolboys. Gunga Ram is a servant in the household where the schoolboys live.

Long Question Answer

Q.1. Justify the title" The Mark of Vishnu" .

Ans. "The Mark of Vishnu" by Khushwant Singh underlines between faith and science. By mentioning Vishnu, an important Hindu god, the author tries to portray faith and tradition in the story. The man Gunga Ram in the story is portrayed as traditional man who had faith in Kala Nag. He believed blindly that the snake would do no harm to him.

However, the snake leads him to his death. Gunga Ram's blind faith and his failure in reasoning the potential threat that a snake possess caused him his death. The mark that the author is talking about is not clearly evident in the story but it might mean the bite mark of the snake. Khushwant might be sarcastically referring to the mark as something given to Gunga Ram by his blind faith.

Q.2. Character Sketch of Gunga Ram ?

Ans. Gunga Ram appears in the short story "The Mark of Vishnu" by Khushwant Singh. He is an old servant and follows the Hindu religion. Although he is a Brahmin, he is uneducated. He worships the Trinity of Brahma, Vishnu, and Siva, in accordance with Hindu beliefs, but he is most devoted to Vishnu. Therefore, he smears a V-mark on his forehead in sandalwood paste.

Gunga Ram is very religious. He believes that all life is sacred, even that of the most dangerous creatures: "He would feed and protect snakes because snakes were the most vile of God's creatures on earth. If you could love them, instead of killing them, you proved your point." However, he is also very superstitious.

Q.3. Character sketch of Schoolboys ?

Ans. The schoolboys are a collective character in the short story "The Mark of Vishnu" by Khushwant Singh. They attend the local high school, so they must be teenagers.

They are proud of the knowledge they acquire at school and look down on Gunga Ram for being uneducated. They constantly make fun of him and "belittle him with their new-fangled ideas". They are rude to him and humiliate him all the time. This shows they feel superior to Gunga Ram because they receive an education and Gunga Ram did not. They are also prejudiced, as they believe Gunga Ram does not deserve respect since he is only a servant: "It was the lot of a servant to be constantly squashed".

CHAPTER EIGHT

Pigeons at Daybreak

By Anita Desai

One of his worst afflictions, Mr Basu thought, was not to be able to read the newspaper himself. To have them read to him by his wife. He watched with fiercely controlled irritation that made the corner of his mouth jerk suddenly upwards and outwards, as she searched for her spectacles through the flat. By the time she found them — on the ledge above the bathing place in the bathroom, of all places: what did she want with her spectacles in there? — she had lost the newspaper. When she found it, it was spotted all over with grease for she had left it beside the stove on which the fish was frying. This reminded her to see to the fish before it was overdone. 'You don't want charred fish for your lunch do you?' she shouted back when he called. I-le sat back then, in his tall- backed cane chair, folded his hands over his stomach and knelt that if he were to open his mouth now, even a slit, it would be to let out a scream of abuse. So he kept it tightly shut.

When she had finally come to the end of that round of bumbling activity, moving from stove to bucket, shelf to table, cupboard to kitchen, she came out on the balcony again, triumphantly carrying with her the newspaper as well as the spectacles. 'So,' she said, 'are you ready to listen to the news now?'

'Now, he said, parting his lips with the sound of tearing paper, 'I'm ready'

But Otima Basu never heard such sounds, such ironies or distressed Quite pleased with all she had accomplished, and at having half an hour in which to sit down comfortably, she settled herself on top of a cane stool like a large soft cushion of white cotton, oiled hair and gold bangles. Humming a little air from the last Hindi film she had seen, she opened out the newspaper on her soft, doughy lap and began to hum out the headlines. In spite of himself, Amul Basu leaned forward, strained his eyes to catch an interesting headline for he simply couldn't believe this was all the papers had to offer.

"'Rice smugglers caught'" she read out, but immediately ran along a train of thought of her own. 'What can they expect? Everyone knows there is enough rice in the land, it's the hoarders and black—marketeers who keep it from us, naturally people will break the law and take to smuggling . . .'

'What else? What else?' Mr Basu snapped at her. 'Nothing else in the papers?'

'Ah — ah — hmm,' she muttered as her eyes roved up and down the columns, looking very round and glassy behind the steel—rimmed spectacles. "'Blue bull menace in Delhi airport can be solved by narcotic 'Blue bulls? Blue bulls?' snorted Mr Basu, almost tipping out of his chair. 'How do you mean, "blue bulls"? What's a blue bull? You can't be reading right.'

'I am reading right,' she protested. 'Think I can't read? Did my B.A. helped two children through school and college, and you think I can't read? Blue bulls it says here, blue bulls it is.'

'Can't be,' he grumbled, but retreated into his chair from her unexpectedly spirited defence. 'Must be a printing mistake. There are bulls, buffaloes, bullocks, and bul-buls, but whoever heard of a blue bull? Nilgai, do they mean? But that creature is nearly extinct. How can there be any at the airport? It's all rot, somebody's fantasy-'

All right, I'll stop reading, if you'd rather. I have enough to do in the kitchen, you know,' she threatened him, but he pressed his lips together and, with a little stab of his hand, beckoned her to pick up the papers and continue.

Ah — ah — hmm. What pictures are on this week, I wonder?' she continued, partly because that was a subject of consuming interest to her and partly because she thought it a safe subject to move onto. 'Teri Meri Kismet — "the heart-warming saga of an unhappy wife". No, no, no. Do Dost — winner of three Filmfare awards — ahh . . .'

'Please, please, Otima, the news,' Mr Basu reminded her.

'Nothing to interest you,' she said but tore herself away from the entertainments column for his sake. "'Anti—arthritis drug" — not your problem. "Betel leaves cause cancer." Hmph. I know at least a hundred people who chew betel leaves and are as fit—'

'All right. All right. What else?'

'What news are you interested in then?' she flared up, but immediately subsided and browsed on, comfortably scratching the sole of her foot as she did so. '"Floods in Assam." "Drought in Maharashtra? When is there not? "Two hundred cholera deaths." "A woman and child have a miraculous escape when their house collapses." "Husband held for murder of wife." See?' she cried excitedly. 'Once more. How often does this happen? "Husband and mother—in—law have been arrested on charge of pouring kerosene on Kantibai's clothes and setting her on fire while she slept." Yes, that is how they always do it. Why? Probably the dowry didn't satisfy them, they must have hoped to get one more.

He groaned and sank back in his chair. He knew there was no stopping her now. Except for stories of grotesque births like those of two—headed children or five—legged calves, there was nothing she loved as dearly as tales of murder and atrocity, and short of his having a stroke or the fish—seller arriving at the door, nothing could distract her now He even heaved himself out of his chair and shuffled off to the other end of the balcony to feed the parrot in its cage a green chilli or two without her so much as noticing his departure. But when she had read to the end of that fascinating item, she ran into another that she read on in a voice like a law—maker's, and he heard it without wishing to "Electricity will be switched off as urgent repairs to power lines must be made, in Darya Ganj and Kashmere Gate area, from 8 p.m. to 6 a.m. on the twenty—first of May." My God, that is today.'

'Today? Tonight? No electricity? he echoed, letting the green chilli fall to the floor of the cage where other offered and refused chillies lay in a rotting heap. 'How will I sleep then?' he gasped fearfully. 'Without a fan? In this heat?' and already his diaphragm seemed to cave in his chest to rise and fall as he panted for breath. Clutching his throat he groped his way back to the cane chair. 'Otima, Otima, I can't breathe!' he moaned.

She put the papers away and rose with a sigh of irritation and anxiety, the kind a sickly child arouses in its tired mother. She herself at fifty—six, had not a wrinkle on her oiled face, scarcely a grey hair on her head. As smooth as butter, as round as a cake, life might still have been delectable to her if it had not been for the asthma that attacked her husband and made him seem, at sixty—one, almost decrepit.

'I'll bring you your inhaler. Don't get worried, just don't get worried,' she told him and bustled off to find his inhaler and cortisone When she held them out to him, he lowered his head into the inhaler like a dying man at the one straw left. He grasped it with frantic hands almost clawing her. She shook her head, watching him. 'Why do you let yourself get so upset?' she asked, cursing herself for having read out that particular piece of news to him. 'It won't be so bad. Many people in the city sleep without electric fans - most do. We'll manage -'

'You'll manage,' he spat at her, 'but I?'

There was no soothing him now. She knew how rapidly he would advance from imagined breathlessness into the first frightening stage of a full—blown attack of asthma. His chest was already heaving, he imagined there was no oxygen left for him to breathe, that his lungs had collapsed and could not take in any air. He stared up at the strings of washing that hung from end to end of the balcony, the overflow of furniture that cluttered it, the listless parrot in its cage, the view of all the other crowded, washing—hung balconies up and down the length of the road, and felt there was no oxygen left in the air. 'Stay out here on the balcony, it's a little cooler than inside,' his wife said calmly and left him to go about her work. But she did it absently. Normally she would have relished bargaining with the fish—seller who come to the door with a beckti, some whiskered black river fish and a little squirming hill of pale pink prawns in his flat basket. But today she made her purchases and paid him off rather quickly — she was in a hurry to return to the balcony. 'All right?' she asked, looking down at her husband sunk into a heap on his chair, shaking with the effort to suck in air. His lips tightened and whitened in silent reply. She sighed and went away to sort out spices in the kitchen, to pour them out of large containers into small containers, to fill those that were empty and empty those that were full, giving everything that came her way a little loving polish with the end of her sari for it was something she loved to do, but she did not stay very long. She worried about her husband. Foolish and unreasonable as he seemed to her in his sickness, she could not quite leave him to his agony, whether real or imagined. When the postman brought them a letter from their son in Bhilai, she read out to him the boy's report on his work in the steel mills. The father said nothing but seemed calmer and she was able, after that, to make him eat a little rice and fish jhol, very lightly prepared, just as the doctor prescribed. 'Lie down now,' she said, sucking at a fish bone as she removed the dishes from the table. 'It's too hot out on the balcony. 'Take some rest.'

'Rest?' he snapped at her, but shuffled off into the bedroom and allowed her to make up his bed with all the pillows and bolsters that kept him in an almost sitting position on the flat wooden bed. He shifted and groaned as she heaped up a bolster here, flattened a cushion there, and said he could not possibly sleep, but she thought he did for she kept an eye on him while she leafed through a heap of film and women's magazines on her side of the bed, and thought his eyes were closed genuinely in sleep and that his breathing was almost as regular as the slow circling of the electric fan above them. The fan needed oiling, it made a disturbing clicking sound with every revolution, but who was there to climb up to it and do the oiling and cleaning? Not so easy to get these things done when one's husband is old and ill, she thought She yawned. She rolled over.

When she brought him his afternoon tea, she asked 'Had a good sleep?' which annoyed him. 'Never slept at all,' he snapped, taking the cup from her hands and spilling some tea. 'How can one sleep if one can't breathe?' he growled, and she turned away with a little smile at his stubbornness. But later that evening he was genuinely ill, choked in a panic at his inability to breathe as well as at the prospect of a hot night without a fan. 'What will I do?' he kept moaning in between violent struggles for air that shook his body and left it limp. 'What will I do?'

'I'll tell you,' she suddenly answered, and wiped the perspiration from her face in relief. 'I'll have your bed taken up on the terrace. I can call Bulu from next door to do it — you can sleep out in the open air tonight, eh? That'll be nice, won't it? That will do you good.' She brightened both at the thought of a night spent in the open air on the terrace, just as they had done when they were younger and climbing up and down stairs was nothing to them, and at the thought of having an excuse to visit the neighbours and having a little chat while getting them to come and carry up a string bed for them. Of course old Basu made a protest and a great fuss and coughed and spat and shook and said he could not possibly move in this condition, or be moved by anyone but she insisted and, ignoring him, went out to make the arrangements.

Basu had not been on the terrace for years. While his wife and Basu led him up the stairs, hauling him up and propping him upright by their shoulders as though he were some lifeless bag containing something fragile and valuable, he tried to think when he had last attempted or achieved what now seemed a tortuous struggle up the step concrete steps to the warped green door at the top.

They had given up sleeping there on summer nights long ago, not so much on account of old age or weak knees, really, but because of their perpetual quarrels with the neighbours on the next terrace, separated from theirs by only a broken wooden trellis. Noisy, inconsiderate people addicted to the radio turned on full blast. At times the man had been drunk and troubled and abused his wife who gave as good as she got it had been intolerable. Otima had urged her husband, night after night, to protest. When he did, they had almost killed him. At least they would have had they managed to cross over to the Basus' terrace which they were physically prevented from doing by their sons and daughters. The next night they had been even more offensive. Finally the Basus had been forced to give in and retreat down the stairs to sleep in their closed, airless room under the relentlessly ticking ceiling fan. At least it was private there. After the Hrst few restless nights they wondered how they had ever put up with the public sleeping outdoors and its disturbances — its 'nuisance', as Otima called it in English, thinking it an effective word.

That had not — he groaned aloud as they led him up over the last step to the green door — been the last visit he had paid to the rooftop. As Bulu kicked open the door — half—witted he may be, but he was burly too and good—natured, like so many half—wits — and the city sky revealed itself, in its dirt—swept greys and mauves, on the same level with them, Basu recalled how, not so many years ago, he had taken his daughter Charu's son by the hand to show him the pigeon roosts on so many of the Darya Ganj rooftops, and pointed out to him a flock of collector's pigeons like so many silk and ivory fans flirting in the sky. The boy had watched in silence, holding onto his grandfather's thumb with tense delight. The memory of it silenced his groans as they lowered him onto the bed they had earlier carried up and spread with his many pillows and bolsters. He sat there, getting back his breath, and thinking of Nikhil. When would he see Nikhil again? What would he not give to have that child hold his thumb again and go for a walk with him!

Punctually at eight o'clock the electricity was switched off, immediately sucking up Darya Ganj into a box of shadows, so that the distant glow of Cannaught Place, still lit up, was emphasized. The horizon was illuminated as by a fire, roasted red. The traffic made long stripes of light up and down the streets below them. Lying back, Basu saw the dome of the sky as absolutely impenetrable, shrouded with summer dust, and it seemed to him as airless as the room below. Nikhil, Nikhil. he wept, as though the child might have helped.

Nor could he find any ease, any comfort on that unaccustomed siting bed (the wooden pallet in their room was of course too heavy to carry up, even for Bulu). He complained that his heavy body sank into it as into a hammock, that the strings cut into him, that he could not turn in that wobbling net in which he was caught like some dying fish, gasping for air. It was no cooler than it had been indoors, he complained — there was not the slightest breeze, and the dust was stifling.

Otima soon lost the light-heartedness that had come to her with the unaccustomed change of scene. She tired of dragging around the pillows and piling up the bolsters, helping him into a sitting position and then lowering him into a horizontal one, bringing him his medicines, fanning him with a palm leaf and eventually of his groans and sobs as well Finally she gave up and collapsed onto her own string bed. Lying them exhausted and sleepless, too distracted by the sound of traffic to sleep. All through the night her husband moaned and gasped for air. Towards dawn it was so bad that she had to get up and massage his chest. When done long and patiently enough, it seemed to relieve him.

'Now lie down for a while, I'll go and get some iced water for your head,' she said, lowering him onto the bed, and went tiredly down the stairs like some bundle of damp washing slowly falling. Her eyes drooped, heavy bags held the tiredness under them.

To her surprise, there was a light on in their flat. Then she heard the ticking of the fan. She had forgotten to turn it off when they were up to the terrace and it seemed the electricity had been switched on again, earlier than they had expected. The relief of it brought her energy back in a bound. She bustled up the stairs. I'll bring him down - he'll get some hours of sleep after all, she told herself.

'It's all right,' she called out as she went up to the terrace again. 'The electricity is on again. Come, I'll help you down — you'll get some sleep in your own bed after all.'

'Leave me alone,' he replied, quite gently.

'Why? Why?' she cried. 'I'll help you. You can get into your own bed, you'll be quite comfortable—'

'Leave me alone,' he said again in that still voice. 'It is cool now'

It was. Morning had stirred up some breeze off the sluggish river Jumna beneath the city walls, and it was carried over the rooftops of the stifled city, pale and fresh and delicate. It brought with it the morning light, as delicate and sweet as the breeze itself, a pure pallor unlike the livid glow of artificial lights. This lifted higher and higher into the down of the sky, diluting the darkness there till it, too, grew pale and gradually shades of blue and mauve tinted it lightly.

The old man lay flat and still, gazing up, his mouth hanging open as if to let it pour into him, as cool and fresh as water.

Then, with a swirl and flutter of feathers, a flock of pigeons hurled upwards and spread out against the dome of the sky — opalescent sunlit like small pearls. They caught the light as they rose, turned brighter till they turned at last into crystals, into prisms of light. Then they disappeared into the soft, deep blue of the morning.

Pigeons at Daybreak SUMMERY

While the story proceeds in a linear fashion in time, from noon on a hot summer day to dawn the next day, there are two flashbacks when the tension and conflict are escalated. One takes place when Otima suggested carrying her husband Mr. Basu to the rooftop terrace with their Neighbor's help to relieve the dire situation of his illness with asthma and no electric ceiling fan that night, Mr. Basu recalled the fight with their quarrelsome neighbors on the terrace many years ago. Another one occurs when Mr. Basu was led to the terrace, he recalled a brief yet meaningful moment with his grandson looking at the pigeons on the terrace. Both flashbacks add depth to the structure as they let readers peep into the back story and a pre-existing world. While the first flashback adds more tension to the plot, the second one introduces one of the themes of the story: the simple beauty and delight in the humdrum and dreary of daily life.

These flashbacks happen naturally as the events in the story flow in "a sequence of causally related events", or "narrative profluence" as identified by John Gardner in "The Art of Fiction". The story starts with Otima reading news to Mr. Basu at lunch, and it proceeds from there to their argument about the news, the news of power outage that night, Mr. Basu's anxiety and fear of not being able to get through the night without the electric fan, his genuine illness at night, Otima's attempt to solve the crisis, the failing of that attempt, and to the resolution – electricity switched on earlier and cool morning providing relief to both Otima and Mr. Basu. One thing leads to another, and the coherence and clarity of the structure keep readers focused to find out what would happen next.

The rising tensions in the narrative also urge readers to turn the pages. When the news of power outage broke out, the story shifts to a higher gear of tension for both characters. Mr. Basu "gasped fearfully... and already his diaphragm seemed to cave in..." and Otima "put the papers away and rose with a sigh of irritation and anxiety." The tension rises to climax when Mr. Basu was carried out to the open terrace, and that seemed not solving the issue at hand. He sobbed, could not find any comfort or ease, "his heavy body sank into it as into a hammock... that he could not turn on that wobbling net in which he was caught like some dying fish, gasping for air." Otima "lost the lightheartedness..." and was exhausted. "Finally she gave up and collapsed onto her own string bed..."

The story's resolution brings changes to Mr. Basu and his wife as both see light when the cooling morning comes. Otima saw light in their flat by surprise as the electricity was turned on earlier and this brought relief and energy back to her. Mr.Basu was relieved by the morning breeze, and morning light – "as delicate and sweet as the breeze itself..."

The characters' slice of daily life and its ordeal in one afternoon and night bring out the themes of the story: old age, illness, marriage, holding on, break-through, and perhaps the most present ones – day and night, darkness and light. The story reaches its crisis point at night and the crisis is resolved at dawn. The cycle of day and night and the contrast of darkness and light are universal. The title of the story hints at the theme of light, and the story ends with the recurring symbol of pigeons "caught the light as they rose, turned brighter till they turned at last into crystals, into prisms of light."

<u>Short Question Answer</u>

Q.1. Discuss the relevance of the title 'Pigeons at Day Break.

Ans. The cycle of day and night and the contrast of darkness and light are universal. The title of the story hints at the theme of light, and the story ends with the recurring symbol of pigeons "caught the light as they rose, turned brighter till they turned at last into crystals, into prisms of light."

Q.2. Assess the equation between the old couple.

Ans. The equation between the old couple is more psychological than emotional nature. The old man suffers from acute asthma and keeps panting for break the time. His affliction has made him self-centred and he never thinks discomfort he is causing to his wife. The wife, on the other hand, fulfils wifely duties sincerely and devotedly. She does everything she can for the course of her ailing husband. He we can give the poor ailing husband some allowance for his irrationality and say that there is a good equation between the old couple.

Q.3. On what note does the story end ?

Ans. The story ends on a symbolical note of mystery and suspense. After passing a restless night, the old man becomes quite calm with the coming of the dawn. He lies flat in his bed. His mouth hangs open and his gaze is turned upward. He tells his wife to leave him along. Just then a flock of pigeons hurtles upwards and spreads out in the blue dome of the sky. It rises higher and higher and disappears eventually. And there the story ends. We are left wondering what has happened to the old man. Perhaps his soul, too, in the manner of the pigeons, has taken flight from this mundane earth.

Q.4. Comment on Anita Desai's prose style, with reference to the story, "pigeons at Daybreak".

Ans. Anita Desai's prose style, as depicted in 'Pigeons at Daybreak' is sombre, reflective and psychoanalytical. Her style is free from any rhetorical flourishes. She writes in a very simple, clear and straightforward style. There are hardly any long winding sentences that the reader has to labour hard to comprehend. Through her writing, she probes the working of the human mind in a very detached and objective manner. She does not pronounce her own conclusion, and lets the reader from his or her own conclusions. In her writing, she deals with common human situations in a completely realistic manner. She lets the reader reflect on these situations, and thus provides food for deep thought.

Long -Answer Type Question

Q.1. Describe Basu's ailment and how he copes up with it?

Ans. Mr Basu, an aged man in his early sixties, suffers from many physical and emotional ailments which include asthma and problems in breathing but sometimes there is imagined breathlessness too when there is lack of sufficient air or oxygen due to intense heat or power cut. This imagined state leads to the frightening stage of a full-blown attack of asthma where he feels as if there were no oxygen left for him to breathe, that his lungs had collapsed and he can not take in any air. Mr Basu copes up with it due to the affectionate care and support of his wife Otima who serves him with complete loyalty and selflessness.

Though he seems foolish and unreasonable to her in his sickness, yet she could not quite leave him to his agony, whether real or imagined. When the postman brings them a letter from their son in Bhilai, she read out to him the boy's report on his work in the steel mills. On hearing the contents of the letter, Mr. Basu becomes calmer and is able to eat and relax properly. When it becomes too hot out on the balcony, she offers to shift him up on the terrace where it is comparatively calmer. She knows it fully well that it is not so easy to get various things done when one's husband is old and ill, yet she is never irritated or impatient. She continues taking care of him with utmost devotion till his last breath.

Q.2. Write down a character sketch of Otima.

Ans. Otima, wife of Mr Basu, is a dedicated lady, who nurses and serves her ailing husband with much care and affection. Pressed with all kinds of household chores and duties, she still manages to take enough care of the moods and demands of her husband without any complaints or regrets. As far as her own personality and character is concerned, at fifty-six years of age, she did not have even a single wrinkle on her oiled face or a grey hair on her head. She seemed as smooth as butter and as round as cake. As a matter of fact, life might still have been enjoyable to her if it had not been for the asthma of her husband that had made him totally dependent on her.

Otima tries to take care of him in every humane way like reading newspaper headlines to him, providing him with all kinds of comforts, shifting him from one place to the other so that he could inhale more air and tending to all his real and imagined ailments with affectionate nursing which include bringing inhaler, shifting to terrace and massaging his body. She consoles him in her own sweet way when he gets upset and does not allow him to lose heart. Though physically it was very exhausting for her and she did feel tired and irritated at times, yet emotionally it gave her much relief and satisfaction to serve her husband in a selfless way. Otima's character reflects the beauty of human relationship and human values in difficult circumstances.

Q.3. Throw light on the theme of the story in about 150 words.

Ans. The present story 'Pigeons at Daybreak' deals with the theme of the tremendous power of family and human relationships, particularly the significance of love and care in times of need and ailments. The story discusses the pace of life of an aged couple living in old Delhi. The old man gets easily irritated due to his illness but his wife is always calm and composed. The story describes the beauty of human relationship against the backdrop of all kinds of day to day pressures.

The old man symbolizes life in the twilight years whereas his small grandson stands for continuity of life in all its zeal and enthusiasm. The pigeons symbolize yearning for freedom which is finally attained by the old man. Desai tries to focus on the problems and personal struggles of contemporary life that her characters must learn to cope up with. She maintains that her primary aim is to discover the truth that often lies submerged beneath the reality. The loyalty with which Otima attends to all the real and imagined problems of ailing husband in addition to all her exhausting daily chores speaks of her deep commitment and sincerity towards human relationships.

CHAPTER NINE

Sentence: Definition & Types

A sentence is the largest unit of any language. In English, it begins with a capital letter and ends with a full-stop, or a question mark, or an exclamation mark.

The sentence is generally defined as a word or a group of words that expresses a thorough idea by giving a statement/order, or asking a question, or exclaiming.

Example:

He is a good boy (statement), Is he a good boy? (question), What a nice weather! (exclaiming).

Ideally, a sentence requires at least one subject and one verb. Sometimes the subject of a sentence can be hidden, but the verb must be visible and present in the sentence. Verb is called the heart of a sentence.

Example:

Do it. (In this sentence, a subject 'you' is hidden but verb 'do' is visible)

"[A sentence is] a group of words, usually containing a verb, that expresses a thought in the form of a statement, question, instruction, or exclamation and starts with a capital letter when written." - (Cambridge Advanced Learner's Dictionary & Thesaurus © Cambridge University Press.)

More Examples of Sentences

In other words, a complete English sentence must have three characteristics:

- First, in written form, a sentence begins with a capital letter and ends with a period (i.e., a full stop) [.], a note of interrogation (i.e., a question mark) [?], or a note of exclamation (i.e., an exclamation mark) [!].

- Second, it must express a complete thought, not fragmented.
- Third, it must contain at least one subject (hidden/visible) and one verb comprising an independent clause. (An independent clause contains an independent subject and verb and expresses a complete thought.)

<u>Types of Sentences</u>

Structurally, sentences are of four types:

1.

Simple sentence

2.

Compound sentence

3.

Complex sentence, and

4.

Compound-complex sentence.

Simple sentence

A simple sentence must have a single clause (a single verb) which is independent, and it cannot take another clause.
Example:
I always wanted to become a writer. (One clause – one verb)

Compound sentence

A compound sentence must have more than one independent clause with no dependent clauses. Some specific conjunctions, punctuation, or both are used to join together these clauses.

Example:

I always wanted to become a writer, and she wanted to become a doctor. (Two independent clauses – two verbs)

Complex sentence

A complex sentence also has more than one clause but of one them must be an independent clause and the other/others must be (a) dependent clause(es). There are also some particular connectors for the clauses of a complex sentence to be connected.

Example:

I know that you always wanted to be a writer. (Here, a dependent clause is followed by a connector and an independent clause. The other way around is also possible.)

Compound-complex sentence

A compound-complex sentence (or complex–compound sentence) is a mixture of the features of compound and complex sentences in one sentence. So, it must contain at least two independent clauses and at least one dependent clause.

Example:

I know that you always wanted to become a writer, but I always wanted to become a doctor. (Here, one dependent clause is followed by a complex connector and two independent clauses with a compound conjunction between them.)

Functionally, sentences are of mainly four types:

1.

   ### *Declarative sentence*

2.

   ### *Imperative sentence*

3.

Interrogative sentence, and

4.
Exclamatory sentence

Declarative sentence:

An assertive sentence (declarative sentence) simply expresses an opinion/ feeling, or makes a statement, or describes things. In other words, it declares something. This type of sentence ends with a period (i.e., a full-stop).
Examples:

- I want to be a good cricketer. (a statement)
- I am very happy today. (a feeling)

Imperative sentence:

We use an imperative sentence to make a request or to give a command. Imperative sentences usually end with a period (i.e., a full stop), but under certain circumstances, it can end with a note of exclamation (i.e., exclamation mark).
Examples:

- Please sit down.
- I need you to sit down now!

Interrogative sentence:

An interrogative sentence asks a question. Interrogative sentences must end with a note of interrogation (i.e., question mark)
Examples:

- When are you going to submit your assignment?
- Do you know him?

Exclamatory sentence.

An exclamatory sentence expresses overflow of emotions. These emotions can be of happiness, wonder, sorrow, anger, etc.

Examples:

- What a day it was!
- I cannot believe he would do that!

CHAPTER TEN

Part of Speech

What is a Part of Speech?

Parts of speech are among the first grammar topics we learn when we are in school or when we start our English language learning process. Parts of speech can be defined as words that perform different roles in a sentence. Some parts of speech can perform the functions of other parts of speech too.

Parts of Speech Definition

The Oxford Learner's Dictionary defines parts of speech as "One of the classes into which words are divided according to their grammar, such as noun, verb, adjective, etc."

The Cambridge Dictionary also gives a similar definition – "One of the grammatical groups into which words are divided, such as noun, verb, and adjective".

Different Parts of Speech with Examples

Parts of speech include nouns, pronouns, verbs, adverbs, adjectives, prepositions, conjunctions and interjections.

8 Parts of Speech Definitions and Examples:

1. Nouns are words that are used to name people, places, animals, ideas and things. Nouns can be classified into two main categories: Common nouns and Proper nouns. Common nouns are generic like ball, car, stick, for instance, and proper nouns are more specific like Charles, The White House, The Sun, etc. Also, Explore Singular Nouns and Plural Nouns.

Examples of nouns used in sentences:

- She bought a pair of shoes. (thing)
- I have a pet. (animal)
- Is this your book? (object)
- Many people have a fear of darkness. (ideas/abstract nouns)
- He is my brother. (person)
- This is my school. (place)

2. Pronouns are words that are used to substitute a noun in a sentence. There are different types of pronouns. Some of them are reflexive pronouns, possessive pronouns, relative pronouns and indefinite pronouns. I, he, she, it, them, his, yours, anyone, nobody, who, where, etc., are some of the pronouns.

Examples of pronouns used in sentences:

- I reached home at six in the evening. (1st person singular pronoun)
- Did someone see a red bag on the counter? (Indefinite pronoun)
- Is this the boy who won the first prize? (Relative pronoun)
- That is my mom. (Possessive pronoun)
- I hurt myself yesterday when we were playing cricket. (Reflexive pronoun)

3. Verbs are words that denote an action that is being performed by the noun or the subject in a sentence. They are also called action words. Some examples of verbs are read, sit, run, pick, garnish, come, pitch, etc.

Examples of verbs used in sentences:

- She plays cricket every day.
- Darshana and Arul are going to the movies.
- My friends visited me last week.
- Did you have your breakfast?
- My name is Meenakshi Kishore.

4. Adverbs are words that are used to provide more information about verbs, adjectives and other adverbs used in a sentence. There are five main types of adverbs, namely, adverbs of manner, adverbs of degree, adverbs of frequency, adverbs of time and adverbs of place. Some examples of adverbs are today, quickly, randomly, early, 10 a.m. etc.

Examples of adverbs used in sentences:

- Did you come here to buy an umbrella? (Adverb of place)
- I did not go to school yesterday as I was sick. (Adverb of time)
- Savio reads the newspaper everyday. (Adverb of frequency)
- Can you please come quickly? (Adverb of manner)
- Tony was so sleepy that he could hardly keep his eyes open during the meeting. (Adverb of degree)

5. Adjectives are words that are used to describe or provide more information about the noun or the subject in a sentence. Some examples of adjectives include good, ugly, quick, beautiful, late, etc.

Examples of adjectives used in sentences:

- The place we visited yesterday was serene.
- Did you see how big that dog was?
- The weather is pleasant today.
- The red dress you wore on your birthday was lovely.
- My brother had only one chapati for breakfast.

6. Prepositions are words that are used to link one part of the sentence to another. Prepositions show the position of the object or subject in a sentence. Some examples of prepositions are in, out, besides, in dront of, below, opposite, etc.

Examples of prepositions used in sentences:

- The teacher asked the students to draw lines on the paper so that they could write in straight lines.
- The child hid his birthday presents under his bed.
- Mom asked me to go to the store near my school.
- The thieves jumped over the wall and escaped before we could reach home.

7. Conjunctions are a part of speech that is used to connect two different parts of a sentence, phrases and clauses. Some examples of conjunctions are and, or, for, yet, although, because, not only, etc.

Examples of conjunctions used in sentences:

- Meera and Jasmine had come to my birthday party.
- Jane did not go to work as she was sick.
- Unless you work hard, you cannot score good marks.
- I have not finished my project yet.

8. Interjections are words that are used to convey strong emotions or feelings. Some examples of interjections are oh, wow, alas, yippee, etc. It is always followed by an exclamation mark.

Examples of interjections used in sentences:

- Wow! What a wonderful work of art.
- Alas! That is really sad.
- Yippee! We won the match.

Sentences with all 8 Parts of Speech

Noun – Tom lives in New York.

Pronoun – Did she find the book she was looking for?

Verb – I reached home.

Adverb – The tea is too hot.

Adjective – The movie was amazing.

Preposition – The candle was kept under the table.

Conjunction – I was at home all day, but I am feeling very tired.

Interjection – Oh! I forgot to turn off the stove.

CHAPTER ELEVEN

Punctuation

There are 14 punctuation marks that are used in the English language. They are: the period, question mark, exclamation point, comma, colon, semicolon, dash, hyphen, brackets, braces, parentheses, apostrophe, quotation mark, and ellipsis.

The 14 Punctuation Marks with Examples

We can break down the punctuation marks into five categories, as follows:

- Sentence endings: period, question mark, exclamation point
- Comma, colon, and semicolon
- Dash and hyphen
- Brackets, braces, and parentheses
- Apostrophe, quotation marks, and ellipsis

Each category serves its own purpose within a sentence or a text. While there are some differences between American and British punctuation styles, here we'll focus on the main examples instead of breaking down the slight differences. Let's take a closer look at each punctuation mark and its usages.

Period (.)

This one is probably the most straightforward. Also referred to as a full stop, the period denotes the end of a sentence. A full sentence is considered as one that is complete and declarative.

Here's an **example** of a period at the end of a sentence:

- The dog ran under the fence.

Periods are also used in abbreviations, such as in names or titles.
Here are **examples** of how to use a period in abbreviations:

- Dr. Smith read his patient's chart.
- Mr. H. Potter opened his front door.

Question Mark (?)

A question mark also ends a sentence, however it ends a sentence that is a direct question. Typically, sentences that are questions begin with what, how, when, where, why, or who.
Here's how to use a question mark in a sentence:

- How do you like your eggs?
- Why didn't you like the movie last night?

Generally, a question mark also denotes a shift in tone in a sentence if it's being read out loud, so this is something to take note of.

Exclamation Point (!)

An exclamation point or exclamation mark is also used at the end of a sentence when that sentence expresses an intense emotion. The expression can be a variety of things, from excitement, disgust, anger, joy, or anything else. Exclamation points are meant to add emphasis to a sentence.
Here's how to use one in a sentence:

- "Look out behind you!" she yelled.
- I'm so excited to go to the park tomorrow!

Comma (,)

Commas are used to insert a pause into a sentence. The purpose of the pause can be for different reasons, such as to separate ideas, phrases, or even alter the structure of a sentence.

Commas have a few different uses. Commas are used for a direct address, such as:

- Joe, it was nice to see you again.

They're also used to separate two complete sentences:

- He went to the library, and then he went out for lunch.

Commas can also be used to list items in a sentence:

- She went shopping and bought shoes, a dress, two shirts, and a pair of pants.

Commas are one of the most misused punctuation points, and its misuse often results in a comma splice. A comma splice is when you join two independent clauses with a comma instead of a conjunction. For example:

- It's almost time for dinner, I'm not hungry.
- Instead of using a comma, the sentence should read:
- It's almost time for dinner and I'm not hungry.

Oxford commas are often debated within academics and the English language, and using one often comes down to preference. An Oxford comma is when a final comma is placed on the last item of a list. For example:

- He likes to eat fruits, cake, vegetables, and pasta.

Colon (:)

A colon has three primary uses. One way to use it is when introducing something, such as a quote, an example, a series, or an explanation.

She took four classes last semester: history, biology, arts, and economics.

A colon can also be used to link two independent clauses if the second clause clarifies or completes the first one. For example:

- They didn't have time to waste: it was already late.
- Finally, a colon can also emphasize a subject in a sentence:
- I only hate one vegetable: brussel sprouts.

Semicolon (;)

Similar to a colon, a semicolon links two independent clauses. However, in this case, the clauses are more closely related than when you would use a colon. For example:

I have a meeting tomorrow morning; I can't go out tonight.

Both clauses are independent enough to be their own sentences, but instead of using a period, it's possible to use a semicolon to show both clauses are connected.

Another less common use for semicolons is within a list that uses commas. Have a look:

- Last summer we traveled to London, England; Paris, France; Rome, Italy; and Athens, Greece.

Dash (-)

There are two types of dashes that vary in size and use.

En dash: Typically shorter in length, the en dash is used to denote a range, such as between numbers or dates. For example:

- The company was operational from 1990-2000.
- He took the Chicago-New York train last night.
- Em dash: this dash is longer, and is sometimes used instead of other punctuation marks, like commas, colons, or parentheses. Here's an example:
- Her answer was clear — Yes!

Hyphen (-)

Not to be confused with a dash, a hyphen is used in compound words when two or more words are connected. Here are some examples of hyphenated words:

- Step-by-step
- Mother-in-law
- Ex-boyfriend

Brackets ([ ])

Brackets are used to clarify something or for technical terms or explanations. It can also be used to clarify a subject when quoting another person or text. For example:

- She [Mrs. Smith] agrees that cats are better than dogs.
- Adam said that "[summer] is my favorite time of year."

Braces ({ })

It's unlikely you'll need to use braces very often unless you're writing a mathematical or technical text. However, it's still good to know so you don't accidentally use them instead of brackets or parentheses. Braces are usually used in operations, for example:

- 6{3x+[28+2]}=xy

Parentheses (( ))

Parentheses are used to supply further details or information or as an aside. Parentheses can often be replaced with commas and the sentence would retain its same meaning. Here's an example:

- Kate (who is Matt's wife) likes to go for walks.

Apostrophe (')

Apostrophes are meant to show that a letter or letters have been omitted and also to indicate the possessive or contractions. It can also be used to pluralize lowercase letters. Here are some examples:

- I've been working from home for 6 months and it's great.
- Rebecca's dog had surgery yesterday.
- All that's left to do is dot the i's and cross the t's.

Quotation Marks (")

Quotation marks are used to denote text, speech, or words spoken by someone else. It is also used to indicate dialogue.

- "I don't like this," said Mark.
- She told him that she "prefers not to think about that."
- Single quotation marks (' '), not to be confused with apostrophes, are often used for a quote within a quote.
- Jill told her mother "Jack ran up the hill and he said he was going to 'fetch a pail of water' before he fell."

Ellipsis (...)

An ellipsis is three periods used together to represent an omission of words or letters. They are often used to jump from one sentence or phrase to another while omitting unnecessary or obvious words. It's also used when quoting someone and unnecessary words are left out.

Here are some examples:

- At midnight, she began to count down: "ten, nine, eight..." and then the ball dropped.
- When Martin Luther King said "I have a dream..." he was talking about civil rights and an end to racism.

CHAPTER TWELVE

Paragraph

Environmental Pollution

Our environment is our assets, we should not lose the charm of the environment by pollution. We should deal with the environment of our earth like our mother because our earth also nurtures us and shelter us. If the climate gets polluted then will it be possible for us to live? The various types of pollution are Water pollution, soil pollution, noise pollution, land pollution, air pollution, etc. The contaminants of the environment are called pollutants.

The main pollutants come from industries because the factories release harmful and poisonous gases in the atmosphere. This the cause of air pollution. The industrial effluents are also dumped into water bodies, causing water pollution. The other pollutant responsible for pollution is the smoke from combustion, greenhouse gasses emission like carbon dioxide which is high in India.

Environmental pollution increases global warming day by day, so the ice in Antarctica is melting and the harmful gases are also emitting and destroying the whole earth. The animals have endangered, the plants are also dying. Cutting of trees is one of the reasons for environmental pollution. So instead of cutting trees, we should plant more and more trees to enhance the beauty of Earth. On 5th June, we celebrate World Environment Day, so not only we Mahotsav trees on that particular day, but we should plant trees whenever we think it is necessary to do.

We should also celebrate Van Mahotsav to spread the news that every individual should plant trees. It is the responsibility and commitment of every soul to preserve and protect our environment from getting polluted. There is another duty also that we have to perform we should not dump the waste materials in the river or seawater. We should burn them, then we will be able to produce biogas.

Social Media as a Popular Mode of Communication

Social media is one of the most general ways of communication and it is growing very quickly. It changes and affects each person in a different way, or ways. Some people argue that social media has a bad influence on children and young adults, and that it depressingly affects their brains, character, or personalities. Most people see that the social media has a more positive effect on them than a negative one. Social media has helped many people around the world to connect, or re-connect, with each other, easily. Social media is essentially the new way of keeping in touch with everything and everyone, and of even strengthening bonds between each other. First of all, social media has made it possible for people, or even families, who live far away from each other to communicate easily. Before, people used to communicate through writing letters and having them sent through the mail, which would take a lot of time and communication, could not be done fast enough and constantly. Another way that communication was done before was by talking through the old-fashioned telephone. Now communication is easily done through social communication network on a daily basis using the Internet.

Facebook is a forge in today's social world. Its allow people to bond with anybody from their best friends to far-away relatives, as well as share their personal thoughts, pictures, videos, blogs and links. Facebook should always be a top priority for higher education marketers. The addition of Facebook Chat bots has also opened up a whole new world in customer service and digital marketing.

Twitter is a fast crammed network that allows users to share their information. It can seem like the next best way to reach prospective students. Take into consideration however, that nearly 79% of Twitter accounts are located outside of the United States. If this doesn't affect your digital marketing strategy, then Twitter can still be a lucrative platform. Just remember that the most important aspect of marketing on Twitter is the hash tag.

Snapchat is a temporary social media, allow user to allocate information that can be only being seen 24 hours atmost. This social media is only available through a mobile app and boast approximately 166 million daily users. This app is designed for tech-savvy and content-hungry users. In other words, Snapchat is the perfect application to reach millennial, especially for universities looking to share a different side of their campus and boost interest in their brand.

Instagram is tremendously admired among younger generations, with 59% of 18-29 year olds using the app. Instagram created similar features for their stories, like filters and stickers, but implemented it in their own unique way. Instagram Stories has become an integral part of this social media app. Along with announcing its one year anniversary, Instagram Stories now has 250 million daily users.

In Social media the truth and reality come together through the social media. The individual messages on social media are constructing as news feeds and is released to the networks and groups. Social media have given the power to bring together truth precisely and spread it as fast as possible. When a news story is shared by the individual on social media other users have the chance to verify the truth and accuracy and discuss the same. This authority to give information through social media has challenge the ability of the prearranged bodies who claimed to be the absolute custodian of truth. Any such attempts to skew the truth by the powerful tools mass media have been neutralized by the all-powerful social media. The days to state power over the public having sway control over the tools of mass communication are over in the age of social media. Technology has given people the ability to digitally detain real time events and share them on social media. The reputation of social media sites like YouTube Facebook etc. is due to real time events posts. This has enable persons to bring the truth to public sphere giving them the power over those who once controlled all such information. Such development is possible only because of the surge in information communication technologies that has catapulted the social media.

Water Scarcity

Water is the basic necessity of every human being. But, water scarcity is a major issue that is rising very rapidly in modern-day India. The problem has become so severe that in many states the groundwater has almost dried up and people have to depend on water supply from other sources. In addition, water is one of the most misused commodities that we still waste. It is the central point of our lives but not the central point of our focus.

In the past, people understand the value of water and plan their lives around it. Moreover, many civilizations bloom and lost on account of water. But, today we have knowledge but we still fail to understand the value of water.

Reason for Water Scarcity in India

Water scarcity is the cause of mismanagement and excess population growth of the water resources. Also, it is a man-made issue that continues to rise. Besides, some of the reasons for water scarcity are:

Wasteful use of water for Agriculture- India is one of the major food growers in the world. That produces tons of quantity of food to feed its population and export the surplus that is left.

In addition, producing this much food requires a lot of water too. The traditional method of irrigation wastes a lot of water due to evaporation, water conveyance, drainage, percolation, and the overuse of groundwater. Besides, most of the areas in India use traditional irrigation techniques that stress the availability of water.

But, the solution to this problem lies in the extensive irrigation techniques such as micro-irrigation in which we provide water to plants and crops using a sprinkler or drip irrigation.

Food, Clothing, Shelter, Power, Data

Once upon a time, the basic needs for a person to live were pretty simple, yet the expectation and realization of those basic needs is a matter that defines society itself. The ability to provide basic needs to their citizens is a yardstick that has been used to gauge the performance of any given community, city, or nation. But what defines a basic need has evolved as society grows more sophisticated and complex.

How granular should we go to define basic needs? That baseline itself can be hard to pin down in a complex society. Breathing, for example, is considered a life need, but until we had to worry about the impact of pollution, the issue hadn't been a significant concern in the past. Water is another thing that people need to live, and has been the grounds for conflict and strife on many occasions throughout history, but is usually treated as a resource than a staple.

Throughout human history the basic needs for life have usually been considered to be simple. Food to eat, clothing to wear, and shelter from the elements. Aside from clothing, food and shelter are the same basic needs that every non-swimming living thing on this planet requires. Without sustenance and a place to sleep and protect oneself from environmental conditions, it is almost impossible to live.

However, even in the earliest days of humanity, this description wasn't completely correct. Even ancient mankind had fire, for example, and without it are barely able to live better than the animals around them. One could make the argument that fire is also a basic human survival need, because humans are animals who use tools to change and make more habitable the world around them. So in reality we should consider the basics to at the minimum include food, clothing, shelter, and fire.

However, once one accepts the fact that by nature humans are defined by their use of tools and technology (however primitive), that opens up the definitions of basic needs a bit more. The need for blades and knives to cut things from wood to meat and defend oneself (as human claws and teeth are kind of pathetic), and other tools for manipulating the environment, are also critical to life. How do you hunt for, dig up, or otherwise procure and prepare the food needed to live?

Tools make mankind

Let's take a look at that frozen guy they found a few years ago in 1991 in the Ötztal Alps. Named Ötzi, and also called the Iceman or the Similaun Man, the Man from Hauslabjoch, the Tyrolean Iceman, and the Hauslabjoch mummy, this well-preserved natural mummy of a man who lived between 3400 and 3100 BCE can tell us a lot about basic human needs in the context of a pre-industrial society.

When found, Ötzi wore a cloak of woven grass, a coat, a belt, a pair of leggings, as well as a loincloth and shoes, all made of leather of different skins. He also

wore a bearskin cap. The shoes (with laces) were so complex, many researchers believe his society was sophisticated enough to have a cobbler who made shoes for others.

Modern needs

A mature society also has advanced needs, and sophisticated ways to address them. Food, clothing, shelter, fire, and tools grow more complex and take on new forms. Food becomes more and more processed, clothing gets chic, shelter becomes buildings, fire becomes electricity, and tools have expanded to include our information-driven societal infrastructure.

Just as Ötzi travelled with the accutroments of what were the human basics of the time, modern humans have their own versions of everything that ancient person was found with. We carry pocket knives, lighters, flashlights, pens, and a plethora of personal tools, as well as the digital devices needed to function in modern society. Just as the Iceman wouldn't be without the means to hunt and create fire, today's member of society cannot function in any real way without personal electronics.

This is no small matter. Many consider televisions, smartphones, and computers specialty items, yet without them in today's world a person is as useless as a primitive human without the tools they needed to survive in their times. Keeping up to date on what is happening, having the ability to interact with others, and being able to communicate and work in a data-driven environment is just as important as having clothes on your back and a roof over your head.

On the tool side, He also had a pouch sewn to his belt that held items like a scraper, drill, flint flake, bone awl, and dried fungus to use as tinder for fire-starting, along with flint and pyrite for creating sparks. To fill out his kit, Ötzi had an unfinished longbow, a quiver made deerskin with stone-tipped and fletched arrows, a copper axe with a wooden handle, and a chert-bladed wood-handled knife.

So now we should really add to the most rudimentary definition of basic human needs, making the basic staples now food, clothing, shelter, fire, and tools. No human can really live as a human without these things, and if they do not have them they cannot properly exist without external maintenance. Without fire and tools, humans are no better than animals, and must live as such.

Save Fuel for Better Environment

Essay On Save Fuel For Better Environment – In this modern-day lifestyle the fuel has become a necessity for all human beings. We use fuel to fulfill our various needs like cooking, manufacturing, to produce building material and many more. Moreover, in the last one or two decade, we have started depending on fuel so much that it has become our basic necessity. So, ultimately we are dependent on fuel either we like it or not.

What is Fossil Fuel?

It is the fuel that we use for our consumption. It is made up of dead remains and fossils of animals and plants that are buried deep inside the surface of the earth. Also, it forms under extreme environmental pressure and heat. Besides, it is found deep inside the surface of the earth.

The LPG (Liquefied Petroleum Gas), CNG (Compressed Natural Gas), Petrol, diesel, kerosene, wood, coal, and natural gases are all fuels.

Since the dawn of industrialization, the amount and speed of consumption of fuels have increased many folds. Most of the industries run and function by consumption of fuel.

Moreover, a large part of electricity production depends on coal.

Saving fuel means saving the environment

The industrialization has badly damaged the ecosystem. The modern-day machine and vehicles have become a symbol of prosperity.

Moreover, they use a large amount of fuel every day. But in the long run, we are not seeing the bigger picture that this is causing a huge burden on the environment and to save the environment we have to undergo sustainable development.

Our environment is badly infected by harmful and toxic gases released by combustion of fuel by vehicles. In addition, this causes many problems like ozone depletion, global warming. These things have become a massive threat to life on earth. As the depletion of the ozone layer increases the number of greenhouse gases which are constantly increasing the temperature of the surface of the earth.

Besides, this these fuel are limited in quantity and at the current rate of use, they would likely to be exhausted in a few decades. Moreover, they will take centuries to regenerate.

Ways to save fuel for a better environment

Today's man has no respect for nature. They waste our natural resources without thinking about the consequences.

Furthermore, there are ways that can help in saving fuel. Firstly, stick to the speed limit as it decreases the consumption of fuel by vehicles. Secondly, turn off your AC whenever not in use as it consumes more fuel. Also, proper maintenance car is necessary so that the car consumes less fuel.

Cooking and reheating of food and beverages consume a lot of fuel as most of people cook food while keeping the utensils open. Besides, we can reduce this use by switching to electric appliances. In addition, the use of good quality wire also saves electricity.

To conclude, if we use the fuel conveniently and sustainably then we can assure the existence of our next generation. Also, sustainable use will likely to help us in saving the environment as it replenishes itself to its original form if not disturbed by external forces.

synonyms and antonyms

Synonyms & Antonyms Words

Word	Synonym	Antonym	Word	Synonym	Antonym
Alleviate	Aggravate	Abate	Abate	Aggravate	Moderate
Abolish	Setup	Abrogate	Allay	Aggravate	Pacify
Authentic	Fictitious	Accurate	Absolve	Compel	Pardon
Axiom	Absurdity	Adage	Awkward	Adroit	Rude
Accord	Discord	Agreement	Adamant	Flexible	Stubborn
Amplify	Lessen	Augment	Abortive	Productive	Vain
Acumen	Stupidity	Awareness	Busy	Idle	Active

WORD	SYNONYMS	ANTONYMS
Huge	big, vast	small, tiny
Humiliate	embarrass, mortify	honor, dignify
Idle	lazy	busy
Immature	childish	mature, adult
Impartial	neutral	prejudiced
Imperative	vital, crucial	unnecessary
Independent	individualistic	dependent, unsure
Insane	mad	sane
Intelligent	clever	ignorant, dense
Internal	interior	external, outer
Irrelevant	immaterial	relevant
Join	connect	separate
Keep	remain, stay	discard
Large	big	small
Least	smallest	most

WORD	SYNONYMS	ANTONYMS
Long	prolonged	short
Magnify	enlarge	reduce, minimize
Maximum	highest	minimum, least
Mean	intend, aim	pleasant, nice
Migrant	immigrant	immovable
Minor	slight, small	major
Negligent	irresponsible	conscientious
Nice	pleasant	unpleasant
Numerous	many	few, scanty
Oblivious	unaware	mindful, aware
Observe	notice	ignore, disregard
Offend	upset	please, delight
Optimistic	positive	pessimistic
Ordinary	usual, normal	unusual
Outstanding	excellent	insignificant